Justice at War

The Men and Ideas That Shaped America's War on Terror

Justice at War

The Men and Ideas That Shaped
America's War on Terror

David Cole

NEW YORK REVIEW BOOKS

New York

THIS IS A NEW YORK REVIEW BOOK

PUBLISHED BY THE NEW YORK REVIEW OF BOOKS

JUSTICE AT WAR:
THE MEN AND IDEAS THAT SHAPED AMERICA'S WAR ON TERROR
by David Cole

This edition published in 2008
in the United States of America by
The New York Review of Books
435 Hudson Street
New York, NY 10014
www.nyrb.com

Library of Congress Cataloging-in-Publication Data

Cole, David, 1958–
    Justice at war: the men and ideas that shaped America's war on terror / by David Cole.
        p. cm. — (New York Review books collections)
    ISBN-13: 978-1-59017-297-1 (alk. paper)
    ISBN-10: 1-59017-297-3 (alk. paper)
1. War on Terrorism, 2001–. 2. United States—Politics and government—2001–.
3. Civil Rights—United States. I. Title.
HV6432.C618 2008
973.931—dc22

                                                                                    2008007222

ISBN 978-1-59017-297-1
Printed in the United States of America on acid-free paper.

1 3 5 7 9 10 8 6 4 2

For my parents,
Douglas and Virginia Cole,
who taught me to love books
and justice in equal measure

Contents

Introduction

AFTER YEARS OF DENIAL AND OBFUSCATION, the Bush administration in February 2008 admitted that it had engaged in the practice of waterboarding, in which interrogators strap a suspect to a board, wrap his mouth and nose in a towel or tape, and pour water over his face until he can no longer breathe and fears he is drowning. Rumors that the CIA had used the tactic on suspects it held in secret prisons established after the terrorist attacks of September 11, 2001, had been circulating for many years, but the Bush administration's response was always twofold: (1) we don't torture; and (2) we can't tell you what we actually do, because that would tip off the enemy. Once it conceded that waterboarding had been used, it vigorously maintained that the tactic had been legal all along. Stephen Bradbury, acting head of the Justice Department's Office of Legal Counsel, told Congress in February 2008 that while waterboarding may be "distressing, uncomfortable, even frightening," it's not torture because it doesn't involve severe physical pain, and doesn't last very long.[1] By this standard, putting a gun in the mouth of a suspect's daughter and telling him you'll pull the trigger if he doesn't talk would also not amount to

---

1. Dan Eggen, "Justice Official Defends Rough CIA Interrogations; Severe, Lasting Pain Is Torture, He Says," *The Washington Post*, February 17, 2008.

torture—distressing and frightening, perhaps, but free of the lasting and severe physical pain the administration claims is necessary for a tactic to qualify as torture. Bradbury insisted that the CIA's version of waterboarding must be distinguished from those used by the Spanish Inquisition or by the Japanese interrogators we convicted of war crimes for waterboarding one of our citizens during World War II. Apparently the CIA "just" made suspects fear they were drowning by temporarily asphyxiating them, while the others got water in their victims' lungs.

Even after its admission, the administration refused to release a 2002 Justice Department memo that is said to have specifically authorized waterboarding (and other coercive interrogation tactics). At Guantánamo, where waterboarding victims are now being held and may someday be tried, the administration continues to classify its interrogation tactics—including waterboarding—as a secret, and has barred any disclosure of those tactics, even to defendants facing military trials in which evidence obtained from harsh interrogations may be highly relevant to the case against them. And in December 2007, the administration admitted that the CIA had destroyed videotapes it had made of the interrogations of two waterboarded suspects.[2]

Anyone who predicted, prior to September 11, that the United States would formally authorize waterboarding as an intelligence-gathering tool would have been dismissed as paranoid or worse. The United States had, after all, played a leading role in the international effort to adopt the 1984 Convention Against Torture and Other Cruel, Inhuman, and Degrading Treatment or Punishment, which, as its title suggests, prohibits both torture and lesser forms of abuse. The US signed the convention in 1988, the Senate ratified it in 1994, and Congress implemented it by, among other things, making torture

---

2. Dan Eggen and Jody Warrick, "CIA Destroyed Videos Showing Interrogations; Harsh Techniques Seen in 2002 Tapes," *The Washington Post*, December 7, 2007.

a federal crime.[3] The State Department's annual "country reports" on human rights violations have condemned tactics that induce fear of drowning as torture when other countries do it.[4]

The instant cliché that "everything changed" when the World Trade Center towers fell is surely an overstatement, but one of the things that did change was the Bush administration's conception of "justice." The administration's approach to waterboarding reflects its broader approach to the rule of law in the wake of the terrorist attacks. It repeatedly invoked not only the actual attacks of September 11 but the specter of an even more devastating future attack with chemical, biological, or nuclear weapons, to justify previously unthinkable security measures. Waterboarding, disappearances into secret prisons, renditions of suspects to countries long condemned for employing torture, indefinite incommunicado detentions without hearings, ethnic profiling, warrantless wiretapping of Americans, widespread sweeps of Arab and Muslim men living in the United States—all were now considered appropriate and necessary tactics for gathering intelligence in order to forestall another attack. The administration seemed to view the law as an obstacle to getting the job done. In this environment, the lawyers' task was essentially to clear the way—either by arguing that the ordinary legal rules did not apply, by creating new ad hoc rules, or by "reinterpreting" the law to permit what had long been forbidden.

The manner in which waterboarding, long treated as torture, became an acceptable and legally authorized form of interrogation illustrates how Justice Department lawyers conformed the law to

---

3. 18 U.S.C. §§ 2340-2340A.

4. See Bureau of Democracy, Human Rights, and Labor, US Department of State, *Country Reports on Human Rights Practices, 2006* (2007), available at www.state.gov/g/drl/rls/hrrpt/ (characterizing "near-drowning" by Sri Lanka as torture); *Country Reports on Human Rights Practices, 1996–1999* (1997–2000), available at www.state.gov/www/global/human_rights/hrp_reports_mainhp.html (characterizing Tunisia's practice of submerging suspect's head in water as torture); *Country Reports on Human Rights Practices, 1999–2004*, available at www.state.gov/g/drl/rls/hrrpt/ (same).

their desires rather than conforming their practices to the law. At the direction of White House Counsel Alberto Gonzales, the Justice Department's Office of Legal Counsel produced a memorandum in August 2002 that defined torture as narrowly as possible in order to free CIA interrogators to use physical coercion without facing criminal sanctions under the federal torture statute.[5] That memo, drafted by OLC lawyer John Yoo, signed by OLC head and now federal judge Jay Bybee, and directed to Gonzales himself, argued that torture was limited to the sort of pain associated with organ failure or death; that even such pain could be inflicted if it wasn't "specifically intended"; that the president, as commander in chief, could not in any event be bound by the criminal ban on torture; and that defenses of "necessity" and "self-defense," which government lawyers generally reject altogether or very narrowly construe, would be expansively conceived and available to any officer who happened to violate the torture ban. The arguments were strained, to say the least, but as subsequent OLC head Jack Goldsmith later explained in his book, *The Terror Presidency*, discussed in the following pages, such memos were essentially "get-out-of-jail-free cards," because the Justice Department would have a hard time prosecuting someone who had followed the advice of the OLC. In fact, Attorney General Michael Mukasey stated in January 2008 that his office would not open a criminal investigation of the newly admitted waterboarding, because the individuals concerned had acted on the advice of the OLC.[6]

When the August 2002 torture memo was leaked to the press, it was roundly condemned, and the Bush administration was forced to

---

5. Office of Legal Counsel, US Justice Dept., Memorandum from Jay S. Bybee, Assistant Attorney General, to Alberto R. Gonzales, Counsel to the President, "Re: Standards of Conduct for Interrogation under 18 U.S.C. §§ 2340-2340A" (August 1, 2002), reprinted in Mark Danner, *Torture and Truth: America, Abu Ghraib, and the War on Terror* (New York Review Books, 2004), p. 115.

6. Dan Eggen, "Justice Dept. 'Cannot' Probe Waterboarding, Mukasey Says," *The Washington Post*, February 8, 2008.

retract it. A new memo was issued in December 2004, on the eve of Alberto Gonzales's confirmation hearing for his nomination as attorney general. That memo defined torture somewhat less narrowly, but continued to insist that in order to be guilty of torture, an interrogator would have to inflict severe and long-lasting physical pain—the very argument Stephen Bradbury used in February 2008 to defend waterboarding. The December 2004 memo opened by declaring that "torture is abhorrent both to American law and values and to international norms," but included a footnote stating that its new interpretation of torture did not call into question the legality of *any* of the tactics authorized on the strength of the 2002 memo.[7] In other words, the memo was largely a publicity stunt—designed to put forward a more acceptable public face, while changing nothing about the United States' underlying practices.

Defining waterboarding out of the torture prohibition, however, was not sufficient to make it legal. The Convention Against Torture proscribes not only torture, but also any "cruel, inhuman, or degrading treatment." To authorize waterboarding, the administration needed to evade this prohibition as well. It did so by concluding that the protection against cruel, inhuman, and degrading treatment simply did not cover foreign nationals held by the United States outside our borders. In other words, it construed an international human rights treaty—predicated on human dignity—to protect only Americans abroad, not foreigners. Like the original torture memo, this interpretation was adopted in secret. It became public only when Alberto Gonzales was asked a question about the prohibition at his confirmation hearing in January 2005.[8]

---

7. Office of Legal Counsel, US Justice Department, "Memorandum Re: Legal Standards Applicable Under 18 U.S.C. §§ 2340-2340A," December 30, 2004, available at fl1.findlaw .com/news.findlaw.com/hdocs/docs/terrorism/dojtorture123004mem.pdf.

8. Human Rights First, "Human Rights First's Analysis of Gonzales' Testimony Before the Senate Judiciary Committee and His Written Answers to Supplemental Questions," January

To read an international human rights treaty as protecting Americans but not other human beings is to contravene the very basis of human rights—namely, that certain rights derive from human dignity itself. Dignity is not dependent on an American passport. When Congress learned of this interpretation, it overwhelmingly rejected it, insisting in what came to be known as the McCain Amendment that the prohibition on cruel, inhuman, and degrading treatment applied to all persons held by US agents, wherever they were held. That, of course, was the convention's proper interpretation all along, but it took a nearly unanimous Congress to confirm the obvious.

There was still one more prohibition that needed the lawyers' creative treatment—the Geneva Conventions. Those conventions, like the Torture Convention, were adopted with substantial support by the United States, and had long been ratified and made binding on US officials. Common Article 3 of the conventions lays out a minimal standard of protections for all detainees held in "non-international armed conflict," and, among other things, prohibits any "cruel," "humiliating," or "degrading" treatment. Under the federal War Crimes Act, any breach of Common Article 3 was a federal felony. The Justice Department could not argue that the Geneva Conventions were not intended to protect other countries' nationals, as that was their principal purpose. Instead, it asserted that the Geneva Conventions were simply inapplicable to the conflict with al-Qaeda. That conflict, it argued, was international in character, not "non-international," and therefore these prohibitions did not apply. The Supreme Court rejected the administration's position in *Hamdan* v. *Rumsfeld*, reasoning—as had the International Committee of the Red Cross—that under the Geneva Conventions, "non-international" covers all conflicts that are not between two nations (literally "inter-national"), and that under that

24, 2005, available at humanrightsfirst.org/us_law/etn/gonzales/statements/hrf_opp_gonz_full_012405.asp.

reading, the conflict with al-Qaeda was "non-international" and Common Article 3 applied.[9] In effect, the *Hamdan* decision established that the administration had authorized the CIA to commit war crimes. The administration's response? An apology? An admission of error? No. It simply lobbied Congress to enact the Military Commissions Act of 2006, which, among other things, watered down the War Crimes Act so that it no longer criminalizes all breaches of Common Article 3, and retroactively immunized from liability those agents who had violated Common Article 3 before the War Crimes Act was watered down.

A similar pattern of evasion has emerged in the administration's approach to wiretapping. The Foreign Intelligence Surveillance Act (FISA) authorizes foreign intelligence wiretaps, but generally only under a court order. In fact, the act makes it a crime to engage in electronic surveillance without a judicial order. Yet President Bush, again entirely in secret, authorized the National Security Agency to conduct warrantless wiretapping of phone calls between citizens in the United States and various suspects abroad, in direct contravention of a criminal law. Rather than asking Congress to amend FISA, the administration simply directed that it be violated behind closed doors. When the existence of this program was leaked to the press, the administration insisted that it had acted lawfully, advancing another strained and attenuated interpretation to claim that what was on its face a crime was in fact fully authorized. ("On NSA Spying: A Letter to Congress," included as an appendix here, demonstrates just how strained the Bush administration's arguments were.)

When a federal court declared the NSA spying program unconstitutional,[10] the administration responded by announcing that it had

---

9. *Hamdan* v. *Rumsfeld*, 126 S. Ct. 2749, 2796 (2006). See Chapter Three, "Why the Court Said No."

10. ACLU v. *Nat'l Sec. Agency/Central Sec. Serv.*, 438 F. Supp. 2d 754 (D. Mich. 2006), vacated and remanded by ACLU v. NSA, 2007 U.S. App. LEXIS 16149 (6th Cir. 2007), cert. denied, 2008 U.S. LEXIS 1226 (February 19, 2008).

terminated the program, and that it would now conduct wiretapping pursuant to FISA, the very statute it had previously argued it could not possibly comply with. When FISA judges subsequently rejected some of the sweeping wiretap requests, the administration claimed that national security would be imperiled if it was not permitted to continue its program, and convinced Congress, in the Protect America Act, to authorize the very warrantless wiretaps it had been illegally conducting previously—but only on a short-term basis. As of this writing, the administration is fighting hard for permanent authorization of warrantless wiretapping and for a grant of retroactive immunity to telecommunications companies who may have violated the law by allowing the NSA to use their facilities for illegal wiretaps.

The pattern is clear: interpret laws, preferably in secret, to permit what they would, on any standard reading, prohibit. When those interpretations are made public, aggressively defend them, regardless of their merit, with the ultimate claim that the actions were undertaken to prevent another terrorist attack—a claim that, after all, could be made in defense of everything the administration has done in the name of security since September 11. If necessary, seek congressional authorization after the fact, preferably with retroactive immunity for all who acted on the administration's bad advice in the first place. The common denominator in the administration's approach has been its treatment of law not as the guiding hand of past generations informed by prior excesses, but as either a hostile force to be evaded or a tool to be manipulated toward the goal of authorizing whatever actions the administration chooses.

This book examines the role that lawyers, legal scholars, and law have played in the "war on terror." In large part, it does so by reviewing the arguments and rationales advanced by key administration lawyers, including Attorneys General John Ashcroft and Alberto Gonzales, Office of Legal Counsel lawyers John Yoo and Jack Goldsmith, and

Counsel to the Vice President David Addington. The first three essays take as their jumping-off point books by or about these central figures. Reading the works of those who made the fateful decisions offers invaluable insight into the motivations and mindsets that drove the administration to undertake a "war on terror" that included at its center an assault on law itself.[11]

Despite the reputed discipline of the Republican Party and the apparent single-mindedness of the Bush administration, lawyers who have worked within the administration do not speak with one voice —at least not after they are freed from the obligations of their formal positions. Some, such as John Yoo and David Addington, are true believers in executive supremacy. Yoo, whose authorship of the Justice Department's controversial and ultimately abandoned August 2002 torture memo will define his ignominious place in history, proudly defends virtually everything the administration has done. Much like President Bush himself, Yoo seems virtually unable to admit a mistake. He is deeply committed to the propriety and necessity of a strong executive, and used his time in government to advance the theories he had developed as an academic on this subject. These views, I argue in "What Bush Wanted to Hear," are ultimately based on as strained a reading of the history of the Constitution's framing as his torture memo was based on a strained reading of the Convention Against Torture.

As Vice President Dick Cheney's principal lawyer and later chief of staff, David Addington favors Cheney's view that all the limitations on executive power adopted since the abuses of the Vietnam War and Watergate eras are profoundly misguided. In Cheney and Addington's view, these reforms put an unconstitutional straitjacket on the

---

11. Each of the essays included here initially appeared in *The New York Review of Books*. They have been modestly updated and revised to take into account subsequent developments. (See page 147 for the original publication dates of each essay.)

executive, depriving it of the flexibility it needs more than ever in the wake of September 11. Addington, Cheney, and Yoo were all deeply committed to a common vision of a strong executive long before the terrorist attacks. Without the attacks, they would likely have been largely frustrated in their attempts to remake constitutional government. But the attacks, and the fear of a follow-up attack, offered them the opportunity to make their vision a reality.

John Ashcroft is, like Yoo, Addington, and Cheney, also a true believer, but one whose beliefs allowed him, on occasion, to stand up to the administration. His view of the world seems deeply colored by his Christian fundamentalism—it is a world sharply divided into black and white, good and evil. Ashcroft, needless to say, is always on the side of good, and therefore he dismisses those who find fault with his initiatives as "only aiding terrorists." This confidence in his own views, however, on occasion made him a dissenting voice in the administration—on military tribunals, on the ability of the criminal justice system to try terrorists, and most famously, on NSA warrantless wiretapping.

By contrast, Alberto Gonzales seems to have no intensely held beliefs. He served instead as the ultimate facilitator. Like John Yoo, he appears never to have said no to the president. But where Yoo's yeses stemmed from his independent ideological conviction that we need a strong executive in the modern era, Gonzales seems to have had no commitments other than to serve his mentor and master, President Bush. Thus it was Gonzales who suggested that the Geneva Conventions be put aside as "quaint." It was Gonzales who commissioned Yoo to draft the torture memo. It was Gonzales who devised the indefensible theory that an international human rights treaty protected Americans abroad but not foreign nationals. And it was Gonzales who accompanied White House Chief of Staff Andrew Card to the George Washington University Hospital to try to cajole Ashcroft, still under sedation from an emergency gallbladder operation, to overturn the consensus view of all the top officials in the Justice Department—including Ashcroft himself before he went into the hospital—that the NSA warrantless wiretapping program was illegal as it was then constituted. Gonzales was ultimately forced to resign, although disturbingly not for the lawless actions he authorized in the war on terror, but for his role in politically driven dismissals of United States attorneys at the beginning of Bush's second term—by no means his most serious abuse.

Perhaps the most complicated lawyer to play a significant part in the Bush administration's war on terror—and talk about it—is Jack Goldsmith, who first served as a high-level lawyer in the Pentagon and then replaced Jay Bybee as head of the Office of Legal Counsel (ironically enough, after John Ashcroft vetoed Yoo for the job because he perceived Yoo, who he called "Dr. Yes," as more loyal to the White House than to the attorney general). Goldsmith is a deeply conservative law professor whose ideological commitments are difficult to distinguish from Addington's and Yoo's. Like them, he believes in a strong executive, and criticizes the reforms on executive power that followed Watergate and the Vietnam War for "strangling" executive initiative and flexibility. Goldsmith also shares Addington and Yoo's disdain for international law and international human rights, which he considers a conspiracy of the weak designed to tie the United States' hands. Yet Goldsmith's tenure as head of the OLC was characterized by repeated run-ins with Addington, often over Goldsmith's decisions either to overturn prior pro-executive opinions authored by Yoo or simply to tell the administration it could not do something it wanted to do. Goldsmith was no human rights hero. After still-undisclosed revisions, he ultimately approved what still appears to have been a criminal NSA warrantless wiretapping program. And though he ordered the withdrawal of the August 2002 torture memo, he did not do so until it became public, and he proudly notes in his book that doing so didn't require any changes in the government's underlying conduct—which we now know included waterboarding. Nonetheless, Goldsmith's battles were so frequent and so freighted that he drafted three resignation letters in just nine months on the job, and claims that he was ultimately driven out by his many conflicts with Addington. Meanwhile, Goldsmith and Yoo, close friends from Yale Law School before September 11, don't speak to each other anymore.

Why would a lawyer who shared Addington and Yoo's worldview nonetheless clash so strongly with both? In the end, what appears to have divided Goldsmith from Addington and Yoo was not politics, but Goldsmith's more limited willingness to bend the law to conform to executive action. Unlike his counterparts, Goldsmith appears to have treated law as a constraint, even where he may have disagreed with it as a policy matter. What is so remarkable is not that Goldsmith took this approach—after all, this is how lawyers are *supposed* to act—but that this stance was so extraordinary in the Bush White House and Justice Department. There are others who appear to fit this mold. William H. Taft IV, legal adviser to the State Department, clashed with Yoo over the Geneva Conventions. Alberto Mora, legal counsel to the Navy, dissented sharply from Defense Secretary Donald Rumsfeld's authorization of coercive interrogation tactics. And Deputy Attorney General James Comey's decision not to approve the NSA spying program precipitated the Ashcroft–Gonzales hospital confrontation. But these men were exceptions to the rule among high-level lawyers dealing with national security in the Bush administration.

Executive branch officials are not the only government actors in the "war on terror." "Why the Court Said No" analyzes the surprisingly resilient role that the Supreme Court has played on matters of security and the rule of law in the wake of September 11. It focuses on the Court's June 2006 decision in *Hamdan* v. *Rumsfeld*, which ruled that the president's military courts violated both federal and international law. *Hamdan* marked the Court's third intervention in a post–September 11 dispute over the status and treatment of "enemy combatants," and the third straight loss for the Bush administration. Like the Court's earlier decisions, *Hamdan* reflected the triumph of law over claims of unchecked executive power. To their credit, the justices insisted that law has a critical role to play, and were willing to enforce it in a time of crisis.

The *Hamdan* decision was particularly important because it established that the Geneva Conventions apply to the conflict with al-Qaeda, directly rejecting the president's position to the contrary. However, the Court's decision ultimately rested on statutory grounds, leaving an open door for Congress to undercut its pronouncements if it chose to give the president the power he had unilaterally taken. In the Military Commissions Act of 2006, Congress did just that. The legality of Congress's action is now pending before the Supreme Court once again. But however the Court rules, the Military Commissions Act reinforces the lesson that individual rights cannot be left to the political process—especially when they are the rights of foreign nationals, who have no voice in that process.

In addition to examining the individuals who crafted the legal framework for the Bush administration's war on terror, several essays focus on the theoretical, political, and jurisprudential ideas that underlie the war on terror. I have already touched on the influential ideas of John Yoo and David Addington. But a change as fundamental as that which has taken place since September 11 in attitudes toward the rule of law cannot be attributed solely to government lawyers. Those who help frame the public debate also play an important role in making such transformations possible. Therefore I have included here reviews of recent books by two of the United States' most prominent contemporary legal scholars and public intellectuals—Richard Posner, a federal judge and law professor at the University of Chicago, and Bruce Ackerman, of Yale Law School. Posner is conservative, the father of the law and economics movement in legal theory. Ackerman is an eloquent and prolific liberal. Despite their differences, both have authored post–September 11 books that, in my estimation, have helped frame the debate in unfortunate terms.

Posner, who tends to see the world in utilitarian cost-benefit terms, reasons that because we face a potentially catastrophic threat, virtually all rights protections are outweighed by our increased need for security. He likens constitutional constraints to a "suicide pact," and largely dismisses them as the fantasies of head-in-the-sand civil libertarians. Courts, in his view, are ill-suited to assess the tradeoffs between liberty and security, and should therefore defer to the political branches. But if rights protections are to be left to an all-things-considered cost-benefit calculus by the president and Congress, that is, to be honored only at the discretion of the political branches, one is left to wonder what value the Constitution serves. The very purpose of a constitution is to identify certain fundamental rights that we do not trust the political process to protect adequately. Individual freedoms during wartime might well be the paradigmatic case in point. As the post– (and pre–) September 11 record demonstrates, neither the president nor Congress is likely to protect liberty, autonomy, or privacy rights when they consider national security to be on the line. Thus Posner's approach simultaneously dismisses principle for pragmatism, writes courts out of the picture, and leaves constitutionalism during "emergencies" to the whim of politicians—thereby virtually assuring that the vulnerable will be left without meaningful safeguards.

Ackerman is a critic of the Bush administration, but for that reason his book may be even more dangerous than Posner's. An avowed liberal, Ackerman nonetheless buys into the need for relatively untrammeled executive power (at least temporarily) in times of emergency. He specifically advocates giving the president emergency power to detain thousands of individuals on no more than "reasonable suspicion." (In an earlier version of his argument, published in the *Yale*

Law Journal, he proposed authorizing preventive detention on no suspicion at all.) Ackerman contends that if we don't give the administration such power in advance, it will take even more power after the next attack. But he offers no reason to believe that granting such emergency power would be effective either in forestalling future threats to our security or in constraining other executive abuses. His proposed remedy, that is, would seem to do little to respond to the problems of security *or* liberty. That a liberal critic of the Bush administration has advocated mass preventive detention nonetheless could easily be cited after the next attack to legitimate such measures—in all likelihood without Ackerman's creative but wholly unrealistic checks.

One of the most difficult, pervasive, and unresolved issues that post–September 11 security demands pose is how to empower government to obtain the intelligence it needs to forestall another major terrorist attack, while preserving privacy from widespread intrusions. "Uncle Sam Is Watching You" examines the USA Patriot Act and other post–September 11 surveillance initiatives, and argues that we need to rethink Fourth Amendment doctrine if we are to preserve our privacy from the dual threats of advancing technology and persistent fear. The Supreme Court has long ruled that we forfeit any constitutional protection for information that we share with another, and that therefore the Constitution permits the government to obtain that information without any objective basis for suspicion, and without any judicial safeguards. The problem is that in the modern era, virtually everything we do generates some computerized data that is shared with a third party—whether it be the phone company, the Internet service provider, the bank, or the credit card company. At the same time, computers have made it possible to gather and transmit data in vast quantities and "mine" it for suspicious patterns of behavior—however "suspicious" is defined. Must we sacrifice our privacy to the modern world, or can we distinguish between Google knowing what we have searched and said, and the government knowing that information?

The Bush administration's trump card in all the post–September 11 security debates is its claim that it is preventing another attack. It is true, of course, that as of March 2008, there has not been another terrorist attack in the United States since the anthrax mailings that followed shortly after September 11. (Over four thousand Americans have died in Iraq, and ten to twenty times that many Iraqi civilians, but that apparently doesn't enter into the administration's calculus.) But has the administration's assault on law in fact made us more secure? "Are We Safer?" shows that there is little evidence that the administration's most controversial initiatives have captured many actual terrorists or disrupted many actual terrorist plots. Some measures, such as rounding up more than five thousand foreign nationals in antiterrorism preventive detention in the first two years after September 11, have come up entirely emptyhanded. Not one of the five thousand stands convicted of a terrorist offense today, and none remain in detention. Our efforts abroad, particularly in Afghanistan and Pakistan, do seem to have captured some real terrorists—including admitted September 11 mastermind Khalid Sheikh Mohammad. But at the same time, the administration has released about 500 of the 775 persons once held at Guantánamo Bay Naval Station, suggesting that perhaps they were not, after all, "the worst of the worst," as the administration initially maintained. The military has yet to complete a single military trial for war crimes, and the Justice Department has yet to identify a single al-Qaeda cell in the United States.

At the same time, many of the administration's security initiatives have sparked deep and widespread international opposition and opprobrium—including the systemic torture at Abu Ghraib, for which no high-level official has yet been held accountable; the disappearances of countless "suspects" into CIA "black sites," where they have been subjected to brutal mistreatment, for which no one, high- or low-level, has been held responsible; the rendition of suspects to Syria, Egypt, Jordan, and other countries that we have long condemned for their reliance on torture; the launching of a preventive war against Iraq, a predominantly Muslim country that did not attack or threaten to attack us; and more generally, the insistence that we can do to other countries' nationals what we would never tolerate being done to our own citizens. These and other measures have not only come up short in terms of security results; they have effectively aided al-Qaeda, by fueling anti-American resentment, inspiring recruits to the terrorists' cause, and making it far more difficult for us to develop positive ties to the Arab and Muslim communities around the world so that we can isolate al-Qaeda from its potential supporters. Our efforts have instead reinforced al-Qaeda's bases of support and breathed new life into its recruitment programs. It ought not be surprising, then, that according to the National Intelligence Estimate, al-Qaeda has now fully reconstituted itself in the border regions of Pakistan.

More than fifty years ago, Francis Biddle, attorney general under President Franklin Delano Roosevelt during World War II, said that "the Constitution has never greatly bothered any wartime President."[12] Whether that statement is true of all presidents, it certainly appears to apply to President Bush in his "war on terror." Perhaps that is to be expected from the president himself. The job of a government lawyer, however, is to be bothered by the Constitution. That document is designed to place law above politics, in recognition that democratic forces, and those who represent them, will often be tempted to ignore principle for what appears in the short term to be pragmatism. Constitutional law insists that we adhere to principle precisely when it appears costly to do so, understanding that over the long term, our interests are better served by adherence to principle than by surrendering to passion or fear. In the wake of September 11, lawyers in the administration and scholars in the academy failed that

---

12. Francis Biddle, *In Brief Authority* (Doubleday, 1962), p. 219.

calling, letting fear of another, even more catastrophic, attack override their commitments to what the Constitution, and this country, stand for at their best. This is that story.

—David Cole, April 2, 2008

I

THE FUNDAMENTALIST AND
THE FACILITATOR

IN THE DAYS AND WEEKS after the terrorist attacks of September 11, 2001, each time Attorney General John Ashcroft made a public appearance he would preface his remarks by announcing how many "suspected terrorists"—many of them foreign nationals picked up on minor immigration violations—the government had detained. By early November, just seven weeks after the attacks, the official number stood at 1,182. Ashcroft's message was clear. The Justice Department had matters under control, and was preventing another attack by keeping more than one thousand suspects off the streets.

In June 2003, the Justice Department's inspector general issued an extensive report on the federal government's treatment of immigrants locked up as "suspected terrorists" following September 11.[1] The report found that in the first year of the investigation of September 11, more than seven hundred foreign nationals had been swept up, often on no charges at all, and placed in preventive detention under immigration law auspices. By order of Attorney General Ashcroft, their identities were kept secret. Also by order of the attorney general,

---

1. US Department of Justice, Office of the Inspector General, *The September 11 Detainees: A Review of the Treatment of Aliens Held on Immigration Charges in Connection with the Investigation of the September 11 Attacks* (June 2003).

more than six hundred of those detained were tried in secret immigration proceedings, closed to members of their families, the public, the press, and even members of Congress. The prisoners were initially held incommunicado, and thereafter limited to one phone call per week. At the Metropolitan Detention Center in Brooklyn, where eighty-four of the prisoners were kept, guards tried to deny them even that right by treating an affirmative response to the question "you doing all right?" as a waiver of their right to make their weekly phone call.

Immigration law permits detention of foreign nationals while they await the outcome of their deportation proceedings, but generally only if there is evidence that they are dangerous or pose a risk of flight. The government lacked such evidence about most of those rounded up on immigration charges after September 11, so it contrived various strategies for delaying the hearings that would reveal how little evidence it had. When detainees were able to get hearings, and immigration judges started ordering some released, Ashcroft issued a regulation permitting his immigration prosecutors to keep detainees in prison despite the judge's release order, simply by filing a notice of appeal—without regard to whether the appeal had any merit. (Several federal courts have since declared that regulation unconstitutional.) When many of the immigrants agreed to leave the US, the Justice Department refused to let them go, keeping them locked up for months without any legitimate basis in immigration regulations while the FBI apparently tried to satisfy itself that they were not terrorists. Many detainees were brutally beaten. Today not one of these over seven hundred detainees stands convicted of a terrorist crime.[2]

---

2. As a cooperating attorney for the Center for Constitutional Rights, I represent pro bono a number of immigrants who were arrested in terrorism roundups following September 11 and who have sued John Ashcroft and others for their mistreatment. See *Turkmen v. Ashcroft*, 2006 U.S. Dist. LEXIS 39170 (EDNY June 14, 2006).

In a similar case alleging abuse of an Arab Muslim immigrant detained in Brooklyn as a terror suspect after September 11—but not charged with any crime related to terrorism—the

The inspector general's report of 2003 was a strong indictment of "the Ashcroft raids." It found not only deliberate and systematic abuses of basic human rights, but also that the sweeps had done nothing to further our security. What was Ashcroft's response? As he told Congress at a hearing on the report, "We make no apologies."

That response perfectly captures John Ashcroft's approach to his job as President Bush's first attorney general. In his public statements he consistently resisted any attempts to engage in reflection, dialogue, debate, or even candid discussion of the difficult trade-offs between liberty and security that were presented in the aftermath of September 11. Instead, he rigidly adopted the most aggressive show of authority, whether or not this actually served our security needs, while ridiculing and challenging the loyalty of those who dared to express concerns about his practices. Above all, he never admitted a mistake.

In February 2005, Ashcroft was replaced by Alberto Gonzales, a man with a very different style. Soft-spoken and polite where Ashcroft was gruff, dismissive, and rude, Gonzales, who served as White House counsel before assuming the post of attorney general, was willing to meet with critics, including representatives from the ACLU, the Center for Constitutional Rights, and the American-Arab Anti-Discrimination Committee. I attended one such meeting on behalf of the Center for Constitutional Rights in 2005. Gonzales admits that liberty and security issues pose difficult questions. He publicly apologized for the apparently partisan-driven firing of eight United States attorneys, admitting, in the passive voice favored by Washington

---

US Court of Appeals for the Second Circuit in 2007 rejected John Ashcroft's motion to dismiss the case. Refuting Ashcroft's argument that the emergency occasioned by September 11 justified his actions, the Court stated:

> The rights that the plaintiff contends were violated do not vary with surrounding circumstances, such as the right not to be subjected to needlessly harsh conditions of confinement, the right to be free from the use of excessive force, and the right not to be subjected to ethnic or religious discrimination. The strength of our system of constitutional rights derives from the steadfast protection of those rights in both normal and unusual times. (*Iqbal v. Hasty*, 2007 U.S. App. LEXIS 13911 (2d Cir. June 14, 2007))

politicians, that "mistakes were made"—even if he couldn't ever quite recall what the mistakes actually were.

A dramatic showdown between Ashcroft and Gonzales in March 2004 suggests, however, that despite outward appearances, Gonzales was even more willing than Ashcroft to do the president's bidding, regardless of concerns about legality. In dramatic testimony before the Senate Judiciary Committee in May 2007, Bush's former deputy attorney general, James Comey, a Republican and by all accounts a straight shooter, described an astounding effort by then White House Counsel Gonzales to get Ashcroft, while Ashcroft was under sedation in intensive care after an emergency gallbladder operation, to approve a National Security Agency warrantless wiretapping program that Ashcroft, Comey, FBI Director Robert Mueller, and Office of Legal Counsel head Jack Goldsmith had all previously concluded was illegal.

Ashcroft had signed off on the NSA wiretapping program repeatedly after its inception in late 2001. But in March 2004, the Justice Department reevaluated the program, and apparently concluded that it was no longer legal (no one has yet disclosed why the department's views changed or what its specific legal concerns were). Ashcroft and Comey discussed this conclusion the day Ashcroft went into the hospital and agreed that the program should not be recertified. But when Comey, as acting attorney general in Ashcroft's absence, informed the White House of that decision, the White House was not willing to take no for an answer. Instead, Gonzales and White House Chief of Staff Andrew Card made a late-night trip to Ashcroft's hospital bed to see if they could get him to override Comey's decision—even though Ashcroft was so sick that Mrs. Ashcroft had forbidden all visitors, and was apparently willing to relent only when she received a personal call from President Bush himself requesting the meeting.

Gonzales and Card did not tell Comey they were going to the hospital, but Mrs. Ashcroft did. Comey raced to the hospital, as did FBI Director Mueller. Comey, who got there first, described Ashcroft as disoriented and "pretty bad off." Nonetheless, when Gonzales and Card arrived a few minutes later, Ashcroft rebuked them, explaining why he thought the program was illegal, and noting that in any event, "that doesn't matter, because I'm not the attorney general." Pointing to Comey, he concluded, "there is the attorney general." Gonzales and Card left empty-handed.

When President Bush reauthorized the program anyway, Comey, Mueller, Goldsmith, and as many as thirty Justice Department officials threatened to resign. They held off only because Ashcroft's chief of staff thought they should wait until Ashcroft was feeling better to see if he wanted to resign as well. Bush headed off the crisis by agreeing to modify the program to address the Justice Department's legal concerns. Even as modified, however, the program was subsequently declared unconstitutional by a federal judge.[3]

The officials who threatened to resign were all Republican political appointees who had approved and carried out numerous aggressive counterterrorism initiatives before this. That these men were so concerned that they contemplated mass resignations was a sharp rebuke of Gonzales's actions. As Comey put it, Gonzales sought to "do an end run around the acting attorney general" and "take advantage of a very sick man who did not have the powers of the attorney general." Perhaps most disturbing of all was the president's decision, with Gonzales's counsel, to continue the program despite the determination of all the top people in his own Justice Department that it was illegal.

Some have suggested that Ashcroft's sedated stand warrants reevaluation of his role in the "war on terror."[4] While he never expressed

---

3. *ACLU* v. *Nat'l Sec. Agency/Central Sec. Serv.*, 438 F. Supp. 2d 754 (D. Mich. 2006), vacated and remanded by *ACLU* v. *NSA*, 2007 U.S. App. LEXIS 16149 (6th Cir. 2007), cert. denied, 2008 U.S. LEXIS 1226 (February 19, 2008). See also the appendix, "On NSA Spying: A Letter to Congress."

4. Peter Baker and Susan Schmidt, "Ashcroft's Complex Tenure at Justice: On Some Issues, He Battled White House," *The Washington Post*, May 20, 2007.

any doubts in public, this incident suggests that on at least one occasion he stood up, under very trying circumstances, to blatant executive overreaching. But the calls for reevaluation are premature. Ashcroft repeatedly approved the illegal NSA wiretapping program, both before and after the March 2004 incident. And in view of the uniform views of his department that the program was illegal as it existed in March 2004, and Ashcroft's formal transfer of official authority to Comey while he was in the hospital, it would have been remarkable had he done anything but say no to Gonzales and Card. In the end, the event says more about Gonzales, who acted underhandedly and possibly unethically, than about Ashcroft, who did only what he was legally required to do.

Still, the hospital encounter does illustrate a telling difference between Gonzales and Ashcroft. Ashcroft was a true believer, lacking any doubt about his principles (whether they were right or wrong). While that trait allowed him to stand up to the president on this occasion, it more often meant that he was the administration's most outspoken advocate of sweeping executive power.

Gonzales, by contrast, was and is at bottom a consummate facilitator, willing to twist the law to serve his boss's ends—whether on torture, detention, wiretapping, or the politicizing of the Justice Department. As far as we know, he never said no. In the end, however, despite their different styles and characters, both men did much to develop and defend a sweeping view of executive power after September 11—what Joe Conason calls "authoritarianism" in *It Can Happen Here*,[5] and what Frederick Schwarz and Aziz Huq call a "monarchical executive" in *Unchecked and Unbalanced*.[6]

* * *

---

5. *It Can Happen Here: Authoritarian Peril in the Age of Bush* (Thomas Dunne/St. Martin's, 2007.

6. *Unchecked and Unbalanced: Presidential Power in a Time of Terror* (New Press, 2007).

Ashcroft oversaw the entire domestic response to the attacks of September 11, and in doing so consistently exploited laws—such as those governing immigration—for purposes they were never designed to serve. He orchestrated the raids described earlier. He directed the drafting and negotiation with Congress of the USA Patriot Act, which simultaneously expanded federal surveillance power while watering down judicial checks on that power. He launched the Special Registration program, a national campaign of ethnic profiling that required all male immigrants from Arab and Muslim countries—some 80,000 men—to report to immigration authorities and be fingerprinted, photographed, and interviewed—regardless of whether there was any other basis for suspicion. He authorized warrantless eavesdropping on communications between prisoners and their attorneys. He relaxed the rules for FBI spying, freeing agents to monitor religious services and public meetings without first establishing any basis for suspicion.

He also approved many prosecutions of alleged "terrorists" that ultimately fizzled once they got to a jury, including those of Sami al-Hussayen, a Saudi student acquitted of charges that he had aided terrorists by posting links to Muslim sermons on his Web site; Sami al-Arian, a Palestinian computer science professor in Florida who was acquitted of charges that he had conspired with Palestine Islamic Jihad to murder Americans; Mohammed Salah and Abdelhaleem Ashqar, acquitted in Chicago of charges that they had illegally raised funds for Hamas; and Abdel-Ilah Elmardoudi and Karim Koubriti, whose convictions for conspiring to provide material support to terrorism were thrown out because the prosecution failed to disclose to the defense evidence that its principal witness had lied on the stand.

In fact, the Justice Department's record in terrorism prosecutions is astonishingly poor. Its conviction rate for terrorism prosecutions between September 11 and 2004 was only 29 percent, compared to a

92 percent conviction rate for felonies generally.[7] None of the 80,000 men called in for Special Registration or the more than 5,000 foreign nationals the administration admitted to detaining in the first two years after September 11 stands convicted of a terrorist crime today. And the FBI has yet to uncover a single al-Qaeda cell in the United States.

In *Never Again*, Ashcroft's account of his years as attorney general, he offers little defense for these measures.[8] But he inadvertently provides some insight into the character that led him to adopt them in the first place. Ashcroft is the son of a Pentecostal minister who until his death anointed his son with oil every time he assumed a public office, in the tradition of the Old Testament kings of Israel. (When Ashcroft became attorney general, his father had died, so Supreme Court Justice Clarence Thomas did the anointing.) He is a member of the Council for National Policy, a five-hundred-member association that Joe Conason calls "the central committee for the religious right," and whose avowed mission, Conason writes, is to turn America into a "Christian nation."

Ashcroft's voting record as a senator received 100 percent ratings from the Christian Coalition and the National Right to Life Committee. He is a professor at Pat Robertson's fundamentalist Regent University. Upon becoming attorney general, Ashcroft instituted a Bible study group session in his Justice Department office every morning. Like Bush, Ashcroft sees the world in fundamentalist terms, with sharp divisions between good and evil. He associated the president with good, and his opposition with evil—whether that opposition was al-Qaeda, Democrats, or civil libertarians. As Supreme Court Justice Oliver Wendell Holmes Jr. once wrote, "If you have no doubt of your premises or your power and want a certain result with all

---

7. For the 29 percent rate, see NYU Center on Law and Security, "Terrorist Trial Report Card," February 2005, p. 3. For the 92 percent rate, see US Department of Justice, Bureau of Justice Statistics, *Compendium of Federal Justice Statistics, 2004* (December 2006), p. 59.

8. *Never Again: Securing America and Restoring Justice* (Center Street, 2006).

your heart you naturally express your wishes in law and sweep away all opposition." Holmes, of course, meant to criticize that approach as unconstitutional; Ashcroft adopted it whole.

Ashcroft seems to equate faith with the denial that there is any basis for ambiguity or doubt. Just as he made no apologies as attorney general, he expresses no regrets in his reflection (if one can really call it that) on his years at the helm of the Justice Department.

He defends the post–September 11 roundups, for example, by claiming that the government "was much more respectful of due process and citizens' rights" than when it interned Japanese-Americans during World War II. That's like defending segregation on the ground that it's better than slavery. In his retelling, Ashcroft sweeps away all inconvenient facts. He does not even mention the inspector general's report documenting systemic abuses, or the telling fact that not one of the foreign nationals he repeatedly described as "terror suspects" was convicted of a terrorist crime. Instead, he simply asserts that "each action taken by the Department of Justice...is carefully drawn to target a narrow class of individuals—terrorists. Our legal powers are targeted at terrorists. Our investigation is focused on terrorists."

His own account, however, refutes his claims about careful targeting. As he puts it, in the aftermath of September 11, "we didn't yet know who the terrorists were, or where we could find them," but "we had to buy time." When you don't know where the terrorists are—if they are indeed in the United States at all—but you lock up thousands of people anyway "to buy time," you are virtually certain to detain many who pose no threat whatever.

Ashcroft's unwillingness to admit mistakes is coupled with the tactic of demonizing and ridiculing his critics. In his first testimony before Congress after September 11, he claimed that those who evoked "phantoms of lost liberty" were "only giving aid to terrorists." In his book he accuses his critics of talking "incessantly about things that didn't exist, people whose rights were supposedly being infringed upon or were supposedly losing their liberties on a whim, or for no reasons at all." But he never addresses a single one of the hundreds of documented cases of just such infringements.

When librarians expressed concern that the Patriot Act authorized the FBI to demand library records on patrons without showing that the patrons were involved in any terrorist or criminal activity, Ashcroft ridiculed their concerns as "breathless reports and baseless hysteria." He publicly derided the librarians for entertaining paranoid visions of FBI agents "in raincoats, dark suits, and sporting sunglasses," interrogating readers about "how far you have gotten on the latest Tom Clancy novel." He insisted that people need fear Patriot Act surveillance only "if you are spending a lot of time surveilling nuclear power plants with your al Qaeda pals" or "if you have caveside dinners with a certain terrorist thug named bin Laden."

In fact, the number of wiretap and search warrants granted annually under the Foreign Intelligence Surveillance Act doubled after passage of the Patriot Act. And from 2003 to 2005, the FBI issued more than 140,000 "national security letters," administrative subpoenas authorized by the Patriot Act that require no judicial approval, that demand the disclosure of phone, e-mail, financial, and other records, and that forbid people served with such letters from talking about them with anyone. These numbers suggest that the government's focus has been a lot less targeted than Ashcroft snidely suggested. In July 2005, one "national security letter" went to a librarians' consortium in Connecticut, and we know about that one only because the consortium violated the accompanying gag order by approaching an ACLU lawyer to ask about its constitutional rights. (A federal court subsequently held unconstitutional the gag order sent with national security letters.)

Ashcroft's fast and loose treatment of the facts whenever they are at odds with his black-and-white worldview is also demonstrated in his attitude toward the 9/11 Commission. One might think that the nation's top law enforcer would have been interested in what a blue-ribbon bipartisan commission engaged in intensive study of our national security apparatus had to say about the causes of the attacks and what the United States might do to prevent another attack. But he treated the commission as an adversary, not an ally. "From the early stages," he writes dismissively,

> it became apparent that on occasion the [9/11 Commission] hearings were not so much about discovering the truth as they were about assessing blame and grandstanding. Before long, the public hearings disintegrated into show trials.

But if anyone is responsible for grandstanding and casting blame, it is Ashcroft himself. When he testified before the commission, he dramatically announced that he had declassified a 1995 memo discussing the "wall" between law enforcement and intelligence agents that was designed to avoid tainting criminal prosecutions with illegally obtained evidence. The memo, Ashcroft noted, was drafted by Jamie Gorelick, a member of the commission and former deputy attorney general in the Clinton administration. Ashcroft claimed that the "wall" was responsible for the FBI's failure to obtain a warrant to search Zaccarias Moussaoui's computer when he was detained the month before September 11. In other words, September 11 was essentially the Clinton administration's fault.

In fact, the "wall" was not created by Gorelick or the Clinton administration, but dated back to the passage of the Foreign Intelligence Surveillance Act in 1978. Shortly before September 11, Ashcroft's own deputy, Larry Thompson, reaffirmed Gorelick's 1995 memo. And both the 9/11 Commission and the Senate Judiciary Committee found that the "wall" had nothing to do with the failure to search Moussaoui's computer.[9]

---

9. The FBI simply did not have enough information about Moussaoui to meet even the relaxed standard for foreign intelligence searches. (They only learned of his al-Qaeda connections

* * *

While Ashcroft clearly had a prominent and vocal part in the expansion of executive power, Alberto Gonzales was equally important in approving, behind the scenes, many of the administration's most troubling practices. Gonzales advised President Bush to deny Geneva Convention protections to al-Qaeda detainees, dismissing the provisions as "quaint" and "obsolete," and warning that adhering to the Geneva Conventions might inhibit intelligence gathering. (The conventions flatly prohibit torture and inhumane treatment of all prisoners.) He commissioned the Justice Department's Office of Legal Counsel to draft the now-infamous "torture" memorandum of August 2002, which was designed to free the CIA to use harshly coercive tactics in interrogations, including waterboarding.

Gonzales advised the president that the international human rights treaty banning "cruel, inhuman, and degrading treatment" of all human beings simply did not apply to foreign nationals held outside US borders—an unfounded and immoral interpretation resoundingly repudiated by Congress when it became public. He helped draft President Bush's initial order establishing military tribunals, in which foreigners accused of terrorist crimes could be tried and executed by military officers on the basis of secret evidence that they could not see or rebut. And as described above, he advised President Bush to authorize the National Security Agency to conduct warrantless wiretapping on Americans, in contravention of a criminal law and the considered view of the Justice Department. The administration was ultimately forced to retreat from every one of these Gonzales-recommended positions, but not before inflicting lasting damage on the United States' reputation throughout the world.

---

after September 11.) See *The 9/11 Commission Report* (Norton, 2004), pp. 273–276; Senate Judiciary Committee, *Interim Report on FBI Oversight in the 107th Congress by the Senate Judiciary Committee: FISA Implementation Failures* (February 2003), pp. 15–17, 20–35.

In view of this record, it is ironic that in the end Gonzales was forced to resign for his involvement in the scandal over the firing of US attorneys. The first two officials to resign over the firings, Kyle Sampson and Monica Goodling, were both aides to Attorney General John Ashcroft first. And the politicizing did not begin with Gonzales; by many accounts it began as soon as Ashcroft assumed office, as political appointees took over the hiring process, which had traditionally been conducted by career attorneys, and began filling positions, particularly in places like the Civil Rights Division, with young lawyers with little relevant legal experience but substantial ties to the right-wing Federalist Society or the Republican National Lawyers Association. While Gonzales should be held accountable for undermining the independence of the Justice Department, in doing so he was for the most part continuing a pattern begun under Ashcroft.[10]

Gonzales has yet to offer an extensive public accounting of his role, and given his asserted memory lapses, he may never do so. During one Senate hearing, he answered questions about the US attorney dismissals with some variant of "I don't recall" sixty-four times.[11] Gonzales was harshly criticized by virtually every member of the Senate Judiciary Committee—Republican and Democrat—but he simply sat there. Whether out of rank incompetence, loyalty to his boss, or both, he took the fall.

Nancy Baker, Joe Conason, and Frederick Schwarz and Aziz Huq all provide valuable critical perspectives on both Ashcroft and Gonzales.

---

10. For a detailed insiders' account of this phenomenon, see *The Erosion of Rights: Declining Civil Rights Enforcement Under the Bush Administration*, edited by William L. Taylor, Dianne M. Piché, Crystal Rosario, and Joseph D. Rich (Citizens' Commission on Civil Rights/Center for American Progress, 2007).

11. Dana Milbank, "Maybe Gonzales Won't Recall His Painful Day on the Hill," *The Washington Post*, April 20, 2007.

In *General Ashcroft*,[12] Baker's careful command of detail makes for a forceful indictment, precisely because she forgoes the kind of rhetorical overstatement and reductionist rhetoric that Ashcroft himself favors. Conason, like Baker, identifies Ashcroft as a principal player in the Bush administration's attack on checks and balances, but his field of vision is broader. He offers pithy insights into each central character in the post–September 11 drama, including Karl Rove, Dick Cheney, Gonzales, David Addington, and John Yoo. (Interestingly, in Conason's telling Bush himself seems less important than any of these figures.) But where Baker offers a relatively objective account, Conason's book sometimes reads like a partisan attack. It is almost as if he sees the world in Ashcroft's mirror—where Ashcroft sees black and white, Conason sees white and black. He writes, for example, that the administration used color-coded security alerts such as "orange" for political purposes and that Bush went to war in Iraq so Republicans could win the 2002 midterm elections. These claims are not supported by evidence, and undermine what is otherwise a well-written account of an administration bent on establishing authoritarian executive power.

Schwarz and Huq's *Unchecked and Unbalanced* provides a more structural critique of executive excess in the post–September 11 era. Presidential aggrandizement, they remind us, was not invented by George W. Bush. In 1975 and 1976, Congress's Church Committee, on which Schwarz served as legal counsel, revealed extensive abuses of executive power during the cold war, including widespread illegal spying on Americans. Schwarz and Huq suggest that the problem is not just that people like Bush, Cheney, Ashcroft, and Gonzales have been in power, but that institutional flaws make it all too easy for such officials to get away with unconstitutional initiatives in times of crisis. The Church Committee diagnosed four such flaws that

---

12. *General Ashcroft: Attorney at War* (University Press of Kansas, 2006).

encouraged the cold war abuses: ambiguous laws and instructions; implicit orders from high officials to violate the law; secrecy; and feeble congressional oversight. Schwarz and Huq demonstrate that despite many post-Watergate reforms, including the Foreign Intelligence Surveillance Act, the same institutional factors are central to understanding the Bush administration's torture, rendition, and warrantless wiretapping policies.

In short, where Conason stresses the actions of power-hungry politicians and enabling lawyers, Schwarz and Huq emphasize the importance of structural features in the organization of our federal government. Both diagnoses capture a significant part of the story. In some sense, we have had the worst of all possible combinations: Ashcroft and Gonzales, not to mention Bush and Cheney, came to power just when they could do the most damage. They arrived in office with strong ideological commitments to unchecked power, and they exercised authority at a time when the concept of restraint was most vulnerable. If Conason's focus on particular politicians and officials is right, we might expect the problems to subside with a new administration. But if, as I believe, Schwarz and Huq's structural criticism is equally if not more correct, the problems will continue, albeit perhaps less acutely, well after President Bush leaves office.

Missing from both analyses is sufficient consideration of the overwhelming political pressure to prevent another terrorist attack that an event like September 11 places on government officials, regardless of party affiliation. While President Bush and his cabinet are fully responsible for the abuses of their ill-defined "war on terror," no serious Democrat presidential candidate in 2004 had the courage to speak out against their illegal practices—the word "torture," for example, rarely if ever was spoken by John Kerry. Democrats felt it was political suicide to voice concern about human rights abuses when the public was demanding protection from another attack.

The central question, then, is how to respond to the pressure for security without assuming excessive power and condoning abuses. The leaders of the Bush administration not only yielded entirely, but often appeared to play up their contempt for human rights, suggesting that only Republicans were tough enough to protect Americans from terror. Ashcroft himself was perhaps the administration's fiercest proponent of what he called the "preventive paradigm," in which dramatic and highly coercive measures—preventive detention, abusive interrogation, and the like—are brought to bear on people not for wrongs they have committed but because of fears, inevitably speculative, of what they might do.

Ashcroft pursued this approach with zeal from the day after September 11, even though he had no idea how it could be sustained over the long term. In *Bush at War*, Bob Woodward recounts a National Security Council meeting on September 12, 2001, in which FBI Director Robert Mueller warned that the government must seek to avoid tainting evidence in order to be able to bring the terrorists' accomplices to justice. According to Woodward, Ashcroft interrupted, saying, "Let's stop the discussion right here.... The chief mission of US law enforcement... is to stop another attack and apprehend any accomplices to terrorists before they hit us again. If we can't bring them to trial, so be it."[13] In his book, Ashcroft admits that "at the time, I wasn't really sure what we would do with the terrorists when we caught them, especially if we couldn't bring them to trial in our country."

The administration listened to Ashcroft. But Mueller was right. If evidence is obtained illegally, through a warrantless wiretap conducted by the NSA, or through an interrogation featuring sleep deprivation, exposure to extreme heat and cold, sexual humiliation, and waterboarding, it cannot be used to hold defendants responsible for their crimes. That is the principal reason why no single trial for war crimes

---

13. Bob Woodward, *Bush at War* (Simon and Schuster, 2002), p. 42.

has been completed at Guantánamo. And if terrorists cannot be tried for their crimes, the government is left to assert the authority to hold them indefinitely without trial, and, at Guantánamo, without even a fair hearing. Ashcroft recognized this trap the day after September 11—and advocated walking right into it.

If we are to prevail against the tactics of terror, we need structural reforms to ensure clear rules, aggressive congressional oversight, and political leaders who are willing to stand up for principle in the face of overwhelming popular pressure. Following September 11, we had none of these. We need to restore them all if we are to make progress in reestablishing the system of checks and balances that Bush, Ashcroft, and Gonzales so aggressively sought to dismantle in the name of our protection.

2

WHAT BUSH WANTED TO HEAR

FEW LAWYERS HAVE HAD MORE INFLUENCE on President Bush's legal policies in the "war on terror" than John Yoo. This is a remarkable feat, because Yoo was not a cabinet official, not a White House lawyer, and not even a senior officer within the Justice Department. He was merely a mid-level attorney in the Justice Department's Office of Legal Counsel with little supervisory authority and no power to enforce laws. Yet by all accounts, Yoo had a hand in virtually every major legal decision involving the US response to the attacks of September 11, and at every point, so far as we know, his advice was virtually always the same—the president can do whatever the president wants.

Yoo's most famous piece of advice was in an August 2002 memorandum stating that the president cannot constitutionally be barred from ordering torture in wartime—even though the United States has signed and ratified a treaty absolutely forbidding torture under all circumstances, and even though Congress has passed a law pursuant to that treaty, which without any exceptions prohibits torture. Yoo reasoned that because the Constitution makes the president the "Commander-in-Chief," no law can restrict the actions he may take in pursuit of war. On this reasoning, the president would be entitled by the Constitution to resort to genocide if he wished.

Yoo is now back in private life, having returned to the law faculty at the University of California at Berkeley. Unlike some other former members of the administration, he seems to have few if any second thoughts about what he did, and has continued to aggressively defend his views. His book *The Powers of War and Peace: The Constitution and Foreign Affairs After 9/11*[1] shows why Yoo was so influential in the Bush administration. It presents exactly the arguments that the president would have wanted to hear. Yoo contends that the president has unilateral authority to initiate wars without congressional approval, and to interpret, terminate, and violate international treaties at will. Indeed, ratified treaties, Yoo believes, cannot be enforced by courts unless Congress enacts additional legislation to implement them. According to this view, Congress's foreign affairs authority is largely limited to enacting domestic legislation and appropriating money. In other words, when it comes to foreign affairs, the president exercises unilateral authority largely unchecked by law—constitutional or international.

Yoo is by no means the first to advance such positions. Many conservatives favor a strong executive, especially when it comes to foreign affairs, and they are generally skeptical about international law. What Yoo offers that is new is an attempt to reconcile these modern-day conservative preferences with an influential conservative theory of constitutional interpretation: the "originalist" approach, which claims that the Constitution must be interpreted according to the specific understandings held by the framers, the ratifiers, and the public when the Constitution and its amendments were drafted.[2]

---

1. University of Chicago Press, 2005.

2. There are, of course, many reasons to question originalism as a theory of constitutional interpretation, chief among them that the framers used general and open-ended language that indicates a desire not to lock in subsequent generations to the specific understandings of the eighteenth century, as Chief Justice John Roberts himself acknowledged in his confirmation hearings. See Ronald Dworkin, "Judge Roberts on Trial," *The New York Review of Books*, October 20, 2005. I assess Yoo's arguments both with respect to the originalist claims he makes and from a more modern perspective.

The problem for originalists who believe in a strong executive and are cynical about international law is that the framers held precisely the opposite views—they were intensely wary of executive power, and as leaders of a new and vulnerable nation, they were eager to ensure that the mutual obligations they had negotiated with other countries would be honored and enforced. During the last two centuries, of course, executive power has greatly expanded in practice; and the attitude of many US leaders toward international law has grown increasingly disrespectful as the relative strength of the US compared to other nations has increased. But these developments are difficult to square with the doctrine of "original intent," which, at least as expressed by Justice Antonin Scalia and other extreme conservatives, largely disregards the development of the law for the past two centuries. Yoo's task is to reconcile the contemporary uses of American power with his belief in original intent. His views prevailed under the Bush administration, and therefore should be examined not only for their cogency and historical accuracy, but for their consequences for US policy in the "war on terror."

War

On its face, the Constitution divides power over foreign affairs. It gives Congress substantial responsibility, especially with respect to war. Congress has the power to raise and regulate the military; to declare war and issue "Letters of Marque and Reprisal," which authorize lesser forms of conflict; to define offenses against the law of nations; and to regulate international commerce. The Senate must confirm all treaties and all appointments of ambassadors. The president is named as the "Commander-in-Chief," and appoints ambassadors and makes treaties subject to the Senate's consent. In addition, the words "executive power" have, since the beginning of

the republic, been regarded as giving the president an implicit authority to represent the nation in foreign affairs.

These divisions of responsibility were conceived for widely recognized historical and philosophical reasons. The Constitution was
drafted following the Revolutionary War, in which the colonies
rebelled against the abuses of the British monarchy, the prototypical
example of an unaccountable executive. The new nation so distrusted
executive power that the first attempt to form a federal government,
the Articles of Confederation, created only a multi-member Conti-
nental Congress, which was in turn dependent on the states for virtually all significant functions, including imposing taxes, regulating
citizens' behavior, raising an army, and going to war. That experiment
failed, so the Constitution's drafters gave Congress more power, and
revived the concept of a branch of government headed by a single
executive. But they insisted on substantial limits on the power of the
new executive branch, and accordingly assigned to Congress strong
powers that had traditionally been viewed as belonging to the executive—including the power to declare war.

Many of the framers passionately defended the decision to deny
the president the power to involve the nation in war. When Pierce
Butler, a member of the Constitutional Convention, proposed giving
the president the power to make war, his proposal was roundly
rejected. George Mason said the president was "not to be trusted"
with the power of war, and that it should be left with Congress as a
way of "clogging rather than facilitating war."[3] James Wilson, another
member, argued that giving Congress the authority to declare war
"will not hurry us into war; it is calculated to guard against it. It will
not be in the power of a single man, or a single body of men, to
involve us in such distress; for the important power of declaring war

---

3. *The Records of the Federal Convention of 1787*, edited by Max Farrand (Yale University
Press, 1911), Vol. 2, p. 319.

is vested in the legislature at large."[4] Even Alexander Hamilton, one of the founders most in favor of strong executive power, said that "the Legislature alone can interrupt [the blessings of peace] by placing the nation in a state of war."[5] As John Hart Ely, former dean of Stanford Law School, has commented, while the original intention of the Founders on many matters is often "obscure to the point of inscrutability," when it comes to war powers "it isn't."[6]

In the face of this evidence, Yoo boldly asserts that a deeper historical inquiry reveals a very different original intention—namely, to endow the president with power over foreign affairs virtually identical to that of the king of England, including the power to initiate wars without congressional authorization. He argues that the power to "declare War" given to Congress was not meant to include the power to begin or authorize a war, but simply the power to state officially that a war was on—a statement that would be "a courtesy to the enemy" and would authorize the executive to exercise various domestic wartime powers. At most, Yoo contends, the clause giving Congress power to "declare War" was meant to require congressional approval for "total war," a term Yoo never defines, but it left to the president the unilateral decision to engage in all lesser hostilities. He quotes dictionaries from the founding period that defined "declare" as "to pronounce" or "to proclaim," not "to commence." He points out that the Constitution did not give Congress the power to "engage in" or to "levy" war, terms used in other constitutional provisions referring to war.[7] And he notes

---

4. *The Debates in the Several State Conventions: On the Adoption of the Federal Constitution*, edited by Jonathan Elliot (Lippincott, 1836), Vol. 2, p. 528.

5. Alexander Hamilton, "Letters of Pacificus No. 1," *The Works of Alexander Hamilton*, edited by Henry Cabot Lodge (Putnam's, 1904), Vol. 4, p. 443.

6. John Hart Ely, *War and Responsibility: Constitutional Lessons of Vietnam and Its Aftermath* (Princeton University Press, 1993), pp. 2–3; see also Peter Irons, *War Powers: How the Imperial Presidency Hijacked the Constitution* (Metropolitan, 2005).

7. Article I, Section 10 limits the states' ability to "engage in War," and Article III defines treason to include "levying War" against the United States.

that unlike some state constitutions of the time, the federal constitution did not require the president to consult Congress before going to war.

All the evidence Yoo cites, however, can be read more convincingly to corroborate the view he seeks to challenge—namely, that the Constitution gave the president only the power, as commander in chief, to carry out defensive wars when the country came under attack, and to direct operations in wars that Congress authorized. British precedent is of limited utility here, since the framers consciously departed from so much of it. Dictionary definitions of "declare" also offer little guidance, since Yoo ignores that there is a world of difference between someone's "declaring" his or her love for wine or Mozart and a sovereign's declaring war. "Declare War" was in fact a legal term of art, and there is evidence that it was used at the time to mean both the commencement of hostilities and a statement officially recognizing that war was ongoing.[8] The use of the word "declare" rather than "levy" or "engage in" simply reflects the division of authority under which the president actually levies—or carries on—the war once it is begun. Indeed, the framers famously substituted "declare" for "make" in enumerating Congress's war powers for just this reason.[9] And the framers had no reason to require the president to consult with Congress before going to war since it was Congress's decision, not the president's.

Most troubling for Yoo's thesis, his account renders the power to "declare War" a meaningless formality. At the time of the Constitution's drafting, a formal "declaration of war" was not necessary for the exercise of war powers under either domestic or international law, so Yoo's hypothesis that the declaration served that purpose fails.

---

8. Michael D. Ramsey, "Textualism and War Powers," *University of Chicago Law Review*, Vol. 69 (Fall 2002), p. 1543.

9. See Farrand, *The Records of the Federal Convention of 1787*, Vol. 2, pp. 318–319 (quoting James Madison explaining that the change was designed to preserve for the president "the power to repel sudden attacks").

Yoo's further suggestion that the clause recognizes a distinction between "total wars," which must be declared, and lesser wars, which need not be, has no historical basis. Despite his ostensible commitment to originalism, Yoo cites no evidence whatever to suggest that any such distinction existed for the founding generation. Nor does he ever explain what the distinction might mean today. And the fact that the text grants Congress both the power to "declare War" and to issue "Letters of Marque and Reprisal" strongly suggests an intent that Congress decide on all forms of military conflict other than repelling attacks. Once these explanations evaporate, all that is left for Yoo's theory of the war clause is that it gives Congress the power to provide a "courtesy to the enemy"—hardly a persuasive refutation of the clear language of the framers quoted above.

Yoo's evidence does not undermine the conclusion that the framers intended Congress to take responsibility for the decision to send the nation into war. But in some sense, arguments against his theory are academic. Modern practice is closer to Yoo's view than to the framers' vision. Beginning with the Korean War, presidents have routinely involved the nation in military conflicts without waiting for Congress to authorize their initiatives. Yoo notes that while the nation has been involved in approximately 125 military conflicts, Congress has declared war only five times. Were the framers lacking in practical judgment when they gave Congress this power?

Yoo claims that since September 11, it is all the more essential that the nation be able to act swiftly and without hesitation, even preemptively, to protect itself. We can't afford to wait around for Congress to figure out what it wants to do. The "war on terror" does not permit democratic deliberation, at least not in advance. And as Yoo repeatedly insists, Congress remains free to cut off funds for any military action that it does not like.

But there is as good reason today as there was when the Constitution was drafted to give Congress the power to authorize military activities. As the framers accurately predicted, presidents have proven much more eager than Congress to involve the nation in wars. It is easier for one person to make up his mind than for a majority of two houses of Congress to agree on a war policy.

Presidents also tend to benefit from war more than members of Congress, by increasing their short-term popularity, by acquiring broader powers over both the civilian economy and the armed forces, and, sometimes, by the historical recognition later accorded them. Moreover, as the Vietnam War illustrated, even when a war becomes extremely unpopular, it is not easy to cut off funds for the troops.

It is true, as Yoo observes, that, since Harry Truman, presidents of both parties have generally resisted the view that they need congressional authorization to commit forces to military conflict. But this attitude is in fact a relatively recent development. While formal declarations of war have been rare, Yoo fails to note that presidents have generally sought congressional authorization for military actions. Until the Korean War, presidents either openly acknowledged that congressional authorization was necessary or offered rationales for why a particular military initiative was an exception to that rule.[10] Thus, the view that Yoo promotes as "original" has in fact been advanced only during the last fifty years, and only by self-interested executives.

This view is particularly disputed by Congress, as can be seen in the 1973 War Powers Resolution, which sought to reaffirm and restore Congress's constitutional role in deciding whether to go to war, and also in the legislative debates that inevitably take place when presidents talk of going to war.[11] As the war in Iraq has painfully underscored, the decision to go to war, especially a war initiated by

---

10. On the evolving history of executive attitudes toward the war power, see W. Taylor Reveley, "Presidential War-Making: Constitutional Prerogative or Usurpation?" *Virginia Law Review*, Vol. 55 (November 1969), pp. 1243, 1257–1265.

11. For a proposal to reinvigorate Congress's powers over military action, see Leslie H. Gelb and Anne-Marie Slaughter, "Declare War," *The Atlantic*, November 2005.

the president without broad international support, can have disastrous consequences; and extricating the country from such a war can be extremely difficult. Were Congress to be eliminated from the initial decision-making process, as Yoo would prefer, the result would almost certainly be even more wars, and more quagmires such as the one in Iraq. On this issue, the framers were persuasive, and it is Yoo who has failed to understand both the checks on executive power they imposed and the reasons they did so.

Treaties

Yoo's interpretation of the treaty power, like his view of the war power, departs dramatically from the text of the Constitution and its traditional understanding. The Constitution's Supremacy Clause explicitly provides that

> all Treaties made, or which shall be made, under the Authority of the United States, shall be the supreme Law of the Land; and the Judges in every State shall be bound thereby.

On the strength of that clause, and statements made about treaties at the time of the framing, it has long been accepted that treaties have the force of law in the United States, create binding obligations, and may be enforced by courts. Indeed, the Supreme Court long ago stated that treaties are "to be regarded . . . as equivalent to an act of the legislature."[12]

In the modern era, Congress often specifies when ratifying a treaty that it should not be enforceable in court until further legislation is enacted. And even without such directives, courts sometimes find treaties not to be judicially enforceable; the US Court of Appeals for

---

12. *Foster v. Neilson*, 27 U.S. 253, 314 (1829).

the D.C. Circuit did so recently in rejecting a Guantánamo detainee's claim that his pending trial in a military tribunal violated the Geneva Conventions.

Yoo would go further, insisting on a presumption against judicial enforcement unless Congress clearly specifies otherwise. On this view, treaties lack the force of law, and become mere political promises, having about as much force as campaign rhetoric. And he further claims that the president has unilateral authority to interpret, reinterpret, and terminate treaties, effectively rendering presidents above the law when it comes to treaties.

To support these revisionist views, Yoo relies heavily and repeatedly on a rigid dichotomy between foreign affairs—which he sees, in the British tradition, as the executive's domain—and domestic matters—which he sees as the province of the legislature. But as we have seen, the Constitution's framers explicitly rejected such a rigid division, giving Congress and the Senate substantial power over functions that the British saw as executive in nature, including the power to make war and treaties, and expressly assigning the judiciary the responsibility to enforce treaties as the "Law of the Land."

If anything, Yoo's historical evidence is even thinner with respect to the treaty power and the Supremacy Clause than it is with respect to the clause on declaring war. As Jack Rakove, one of the foremost historians of the federal period, has concluded, the framers "were virtually of one mind when it came to giving treaties the status of law."[13] As other historians have pointed out, one of the principal incentives for convening

---

13. Jack Rakove, "Solving a Constitutional Puzzle: The Treatymaking Clause as a Case Study," *Perspectives in American History*, edited by Bernard Bailyn et al. (Cambridge University Press, 1984), Vol. 1, pp. 233, 264. Carlos Vazquez and Martin Flaherty have refuted in persuasive and painstaking detail every aspect of Yoo's argument on the status of treaties. See Carlos Manuel Vazquez, "Laughing at Treaties," *Columbia Law Review*, Vol. 99 (1999), p. 2154; Martin Flaherty, "History Right?: Historical Scholarship, Original Understanding, and Treaties as 'Supreme Law of the Land,'" *Columbia Law Review*, Vol. 99 (1999), p. 2095.

the Constitutional Convention was the embarrassing refusal of state governments to enforce treaties. The Supremacy Clause solved that problem in as direct a way as possible—by making treaties the "Law of the Land," enforceable in courts and binding on government and citizenry alike. That treaties were not thought to need further implementing is underscored by the framers' unanimous decision to omit treaty enforcement from Congress's enumerated powers, "as being superfluous since treaties were to be 'laws.'"[14] Yoo's account turns that conclusion on its head; his reading would render superfluous the Supremacy Clause's assertion that treaties are laws. If treaties had domestic force only when implemented by a subsequent statute, as Yoo maintains, then the statute itself would have the status of the "Law of the Land," not the treaty.

Yoo is no more convincing with respect to presidential interpretation of treaties. He maintains that because foreign policy is an executive prerogative, the executive must be able to reinterpret and terminate treaties unilaterally. But while the Constitution plainly envisioned the president as the principal negotiator of treaties, it also gave clear responsibilities for treaties to the other branches; all treaties must be approved by two thirds of the Senate, and once ratified, treaties become "law" enforceable by the courts. The president must certainly be able to interpret treaties in order to "execute" the laws, just as he must be able to interpret statutes for that purpose. But there is no reason why his interpretations of treaties should be any more binding on courts or the legislature than his interpretations of statutes.

The Rule of Law

Yoo's views on the war and treaty powers share two features. First, they both depart radically from the text of the Constitution. He would

---

14. Farrand, *The Records of the Federal Convention of 1787*, Vol. 2, pp. 389–390.

reduce the power to "declare War" to a mere formality, a courtesy to the enemy; and he would render entirely superfluous the Supremacy Clause's provision that treaties are the "Law of the Land." It is ironic that a president who proclaims his faith in "strict construction" of the Constitution would have found Yoo's interpretations so persuasive, for Yoo is anything but a strict constructionist. One of the arguments most often made in defense of "originalism" is that interpretations emphasizing a "living" or evolving Constitution are too open-ended, and accordingly they permit judges to stray too far from the text. Yoo unwittingly demonstrates that his brand of originalism is just as vulnerable to that criticism as other approaches, if not more so. He not only departs from the text, but contradicts the principles that underlie it.

Second, and more significantly, all of Yoo's departures from the text of the Constitution point in one direction—toward eliminating legal checks on presidential power over foreign affairs. He is candid about this, and defends his theory on the ground that it preserves "flexibility" for the executive in foreign affairs. But the specific "flexibility" he seeks to preserve is the flexibility to involve the nation in war without congressional approval, and to ignore and violate international commitments with impunity. As Carlos Vazquez, a professor of law at Georgetown, has argued in response to Yoo, "flexibility has its benefits, but so does precommitment." The Constitution committed the nation to a legal regime that would make it difficult to go to war and that would provide reliable enforcement of international obligations. Yoo would dispense with both in the name of letting the president have his way.

Even if Yoo is wrong about the original understanding in 1787, is he wrong about the needs of today? As the subtitle of his book indicates, his argument rests not just on revisionist history, but also on arguments about what is practically necessary in a twenty-first-century world threatened by terrorism and weapons of mass destruction. He contends that these developments demand that the president have the leeway to insulate his foreign policy decisions both from the will of Congress and from the demands of international law.

Here it is worth reviewing the positions Yoo advocated while in the executive branch and since, and their consequences in the "war on terror." At every turn, Yoo sought to exploit the "flexibility" he finds in the Constitution to advocate an approach to the "war on terror" in which legal limits are either interpreted away or rejected outright. Just two weeks after the September 11 attacks, Yoo sent an extensive memo to Tim Flanigan, deputy White House counsel, arguing that the president had unilateral authority to use military force not only against the terrorists responsible for the September 11 attacks but against terrorists anywhere on the globe, with or without congressional authorization.[15]

Yoo followed that opinion with a series of memos in January 2002 maintaining, against the strong objections of the State Department, that the Geneva Conventions should not be applied to any detainees captured in the conflict in Afghanistan.[16] Yoo argued that the president could unilaterally suspend the conventions; that al-Qaeda was not party to the treaty; that Afghanistan was a "failed state" and therefore the president could ignore the fact that it had signed the conventions; and that the Taliban had failed to adhere to the requirements of the Geneva Conventions regarding the conduct of war and therefore deserved no protection. Nor, he argued, was the president bound by customary international law, which insists on humane treatment for all wartime detainees. Relying on Yoo's reasoning, the Bush administration claimed that it could capture and detain any person who the president said was a member or supporter of al-Qaeda or

---

15. Memo from John Yoo to Timothy Flanigan, "Re: Memorandum Opinion for the Deputy Counsel to the President," September 25, 2001.

16. These memos, and the State Department responses to them, can be found on the *New Yorker* Web site, www.newyorker.com/online/content/articles/050214on_onlineonly02.

the Taliban, and could categorically deny all detainees the protections of the Geneva Conventions, including a hearing to permit them to challenge their status and restrictions on inhumane interrogation practices.

Echoing Yoo, Alberto Gonzales, then White House counsel, argued at the time that one of the principal reasons for denying detainees protection under the Geneva Conventions was to "preserve flexibility" and make it easier to "quickly obtain information from captured terrorists and their sponsors."[17] When CIA officials reportedly raised concerns that the methods they were using to interrogate high-level al-Qaeda detainees—such as waterboarding—might subject them to criminal liability, Yoo was again consulted. In response, he drafted the August 1, 2002, torture memo, signed by his superior, Jay Bybee, and delivered to Gonzales. In that memo, Yoo "interpreted" the criminal and international law bans on torture in as narrow and legalistic a way as possible; his evident purpose was to allow government officials to use as much coercion as possible in interrogations.

Yoo wrote that threats of death are permissible if they do not threaten "imminent death," and that drugs designed to disrupt the personality may be administered so long as they do not "penetrate to the core of an individual's ability to perceive the world around him." He said that the law prohibiting torture did not prevent interrogators from inflicting mental harm so long as it was not "prolonged." Physical pain could be inflicted so long as it was less severe than the pain associated with "serious physical injury, such as organ failure, impairment of bodily function, or even death."[18]

---

17. Memo from Alberto Gonzales to President Bush, "Decision Re: Application of the Geneva Convention on Prisoners of War to the Conflict With al Qaeda and the Taliban," January 25, 2002.

18. Memo from Jay Bybee to Alberto Gonzales, "Re: Standards of Conduct for Interrogation under 18 U.S.C. §§ 2340-2340A," August 1, 2002. While this memo is signed by Bybee, Yoo has acknowledged that he drafted it.

Even this interpretation did not preserve enough executive "flexibility" for Yoo. In a separate section of the memo, he argued that if these loopholes were not sufficient, the president was free to order outright torture. Any law limiting the president's authority to order torture during wartime, the memo claimed, would "violate the Constitution's sole vesting of the Commander-in-Chief authority in the President."[19]

Since leaving the Justice Department, Yoo has also defended the practice of "extraordinary renditions," in which the United States has kidnapped numerous "suspects" in the war on terror and "rendered" them to third countries with records of torturing detainees.[20] He has argued that the federal courts have no right to review actions by the president that are said to violate the War Powers Clause.[21] And he has defended the practice of targeted assassinations, otherwise known as "summary executions."[22]

In short, the flexibility Yoo advocates allows the administration to lock up human beings indefinitely without charges or hearings, to subject them to brutally coercive interrogation tactics, to send them to other countries with a record of doing worse, to assassinate persons it describes as the enemy without trial, and to keep the courts from interfering with all such actions.

Has such flexibility actually aided the US in dealing with terrorism? In all likelihood, the policies and attitudes Yoo has advanced have made the country less secure. The abuses at Guantánamo and Abu Ghraib have become international embarrassments for the United States, and by many accounts have helped to recruit young

---

19. Memo from Jay Bybee to Alberto Gonzales, "Re: Standards of Conduct for Interrogation under 18 U.S.C. §§ 2340-2340A," August 1, 2002.

20. John Yoo, "Transferring Terrorists," *Notre Dame Law Review*, Vol. 79, No. 4, p. 1183 (2004).

21. John Yoo, "Judicial Review and the War on Terrorism," *George Washington University Law Review*, Vol. 72, No. 1/2, available at ssrn.com/abstract=461721.

22. John Yoo, "Assassination or War?" *San Francisco Chronicle*, September 18, 2005.

people to join al-Qaeda. The US has squandered the sympathy it had on September 12, 2001, and we now find ourselves in a world perhaps more hostile than ever before.

With respect to detainees, thanks to Yoo, the US is now in an untenable bind: on the one hand, it has become increasingly unacceptable for the US to hold hundreds of prisoners indefinitely without trying them; on the other hand our coercive and inhumane interrogation tactics have effectively granted many of the prisoners immunity from trial. Because the evidence we might use against them is tainted by their mistreatment, trials would likely turn into occasions for exposing the United States' brutal interrogation tactics. This predicament was entirely avoidable. Had we given alleged al-Qaeda detainees the fair hearings required by the Geneva Conventions at the outset, and had we conducted humane interrogations at Guantánamo, Abu Ghraib, Camp Mercury, and elsewhere, few would have objected to the US holding some detainees for the duration of the military conflict, and we could have tried those responsible for war crimes. What has been so objectionable to many in the US and abroad is the government's refusal to accept even the limited constraints of the laws of war.

The consequences of Yoo's vaunted "flexibility" have been self-destructive for the US—we have turned a world in which international law was on our side into one in which we see it as our enemy. The Pentagon's National Defense Strategy, issued in March 2005, states:

> Our strength as a nation state will continue to be challenged by those who employ a strategy of the weak, using international fora, judicial processes, and terrorism.

The proposition that judicial processes—the very essence of the rule of law—are to be dismissed as a strategy of the weak, akin to terrorism, suggests the continuing strength of Yoo's influence. When the rule of law is seen simply as a device used by terrorists, something has gone perilously wrong. Michael Ignatieff has written that "it is the very nature of a democracy that it not only does, but should, fight with one hand tied behind its back. It is also in the nature of democracy that it prevails against its enemies precisely because it does."[23] Yoo persuaded the Bush administration to untie its hand and abandon the constraints of the rule of law. Perhaps that is why we are not prevailing.

---

23. Michael Ignatieff, *The Lesser Evil: Political Ethics in an Age of Terror* (Princeton University Press, 2004), p. 24.

3

CONFRONTING CHENEY'S CHENEY

PERHAPS THE MOST POWERFUL LAWYER in the Bush administration is also the most reclusive. David Addington, who was Vice President Dick Cheney's counsel from 2001 to 2005, and since then his chief of staff, does not talk to the press. His voice, however, has been enormously influential behind closed doors, where, with Cheney's backing, he has helped shape the administration's strategy in the war on terror, and in particular its aggressively expansive conception of executive power. Sometimes called "Cheney's Cheney," Addington has twenty years of experience in national security matters—he has been a lawyer for the CIA, for the secretary of defense, and for two congressional committees concerned with intelligence and foreign affairs. He is a prodigious worker, and by all accounts a brilliant inside political player. Richard Shiffrin, deputy general counsel for intelligence at the Defense Department until 2003, called him "an unopposable force."[1] Yet most of the American public has never heard him speak.

Addington's combination of public silence and private power makes him an apt symbol for the Bush administration's general approach to national security. Many of the administration's most controversial policies have been adopted in secret, under Addington's

---

1. See Jane Mayer, "The Hidden Power," *The New Yorker*, July 3, 2006.

direction, often without much input from other parts of the executive branch, much less other branches of government, and without public accountability. Among the measures we know about are disappearances of detainees into secret CIA prisons, the use of torture to gather evidence, rendition of suspects to countries known for torture, and warrantless wiretapping of Americans.

When the public learns of such practices, usually because someone—presumably not David Addington—has leaked information about them to the press, the administration continues to invoke secrecy to block efforts to hold it to account. After *The New York Times* revealed that President Bush had authorized the National Security Agency (NSA) to monitor Americans' phone calls without judicial approval, in violation of a criminal statute, the administration labeled the program a "state secret" and argued that lawsuits challenging its legality must be dismissed in deference to executive claims of confidentiality.[2] On the same grounds, the Supreme Court in October 2007 declined without comment to hear a lawsuit challenging the administration's abduction of an innocent German citizen who was taken to Afghanistan to be tortured, and then dumped on a remote Albanian roadside when US officials realized they had kidnapped the wrong man. The administration argued that the litigation would reveal classified information, and the Supreme Court was unwilling even to consider whether it is consistent with our democratic system to elevate secrecy over all other constitutional and human rights values—including the right not to be tortured.

Because of this secrecy, what little the public knows about Addington and the policies he has advocated necessarily comes from others. No one has provided more credible detail on that subject than Jack Goldsmith, himself a former Bush administration insider, now a Harvard law professor, who has written *The Terror Presidency: Law and*

---

2. I am co-counsel in one such case, *Center for Constitutional Rights v. Bush*.

Judgment Inside the Bush Administration,[3] a captivating memoir of his brief time as head of the Justice Department's Office of Legal Counsel (OLC) under Attorney General John Ashcroft. Goldsmith's repeated run-ins with Addington ultimately drove him from office only nine months after he took the post in October 2003.

Goldsmith's confrontations with Addington are central to the story he tells. They began in his first weeks on the job, when Goldsmith informed Addington that according to his analysis of the law, the Geneva Conventions protect all Iraqis in Iraq, even those we suspect are terrorists. "The President," Addington objected, "has already decided that terrorists do not receive Geneva Convention protections. You cannot question his decision." When Goldsmith told Addington that he did not believe that a surveillance program being conducted by the NSA was legal, Addington replied, "If you rule that way, the blood of the hundred thousand people who die in the next attack will be on *your* hands."

In a discussion about whether surveillance of communications had to be approved by a court, as required by the Foreign Intelligence Surveillance Act (FISA), Addington boasted, "We're one bomb away from getting rid of that obnoxious [FISA] court." And when Goldsmith and other high-level Justice and State Department officials recommended going to Congress to obtain legislative authority for the detention program at Guantánamo Bay, Addington asked dismissively, "Why are you trying to give away the President's power?" As Addington articulated the administration's general strategy, "We're going to push and push and push until some larger force makes us stop."

Goldsmith writes that Addington and Cheney viewed executive power reductively as the "absence of constraint," and rejected all efforts to exercise authority through persuasion, consultation, and

---

3. Norton, 2007.

consensus-building. Such initiatives, they felt, would only show weakness. They bristled at any law that tied the executive's hands. As Goldsmith tells it, Addington and Cheney

> dealt with FISA the way they dealt with other laws they didn't like: they blew through them in secret based on flimsy legal opinions that they guarded closely so no one could question the legal basis for the operations.

Addington would not even let the National Security Agency's counsel see the opinions purporting to authorize NSA spying. And when other officials objected that a particular policy would hurt the United States' image with its allies, Addington's response was even more dismissive; according to Goldsmith, he invariably replied, "They don't have a vote."

Goldsmith's account is credible not only because he was an insider, but because he shares so many of Addington's views. Like his classmate at Yale Law School and onetime friend John Yoo, another Office of Legal Counsel lawyer who worked closely with Addington to justify the administration's most extreme assertions of unilateral power, Goldsmith made his reputation as a scholar with articles highly skeptical of international law, human rights, and international institutions. While serving in the legal counsel office at the Department of Defense, he wrote a memo for Donald Rumsfeld dismissing international law as a tool of the weak. He accused other nations and nongovernmental organizations of creating a "web of international laws and judicial institutions that today threatens USG interests," and recommended that the United States "confront... the threat." And Goldsmith is equally critical of domestic legal constraints; in *The Terror Presidency* he characterizes post-Watergate legal limits on executive power—the very limits Addington and Cheney so resented—as "one of the Bush administration's biggest obstacles in responding to the 9/11 attacks."

Why, then, did two lawyers with so much in common come to such an impasse? In Goldsmith's retelling, it is because he was more faithful to the law than to the president, and was unwilling to bend the law at every juncture to authorize whatever the administration desired. Apparently, Goldsmith was the first official in the OLC to challenge the administration's claims to unchecked power. While other high officials, including Secretary of State Colin Powell, State Department legal adviser William Taft III, and National Security Council adviser John Bellinger, had objected to various aspects of the war on terror, they could be, and generally were, ignored. It was more difficult to disregard the OLC, because its job is to interpret federal law within the executive branch. If it takes the view that an administration program is legal, those charged with carrying it out can rest assured that they will not be prosecuted for violating federal law. As Goldsmith puts it, the OLC has the power to issue "get-out-of-jail-free cards." Because the White House was repeatedly pushing the limits of criminal law on torture, wiretapping, and war crimes, it deemed opposition from the OLC unacceptable. And after his appointment on October 6, 2003, Goldsmith soon showed that, unlike his predecessor, Jay S. Bybee, he was willing to say "no."

Goldsmith crossed the administration frequently. As noted above, he ruled that the Geneva Conventions protect all Iraqi civilians, much to Addington's displeasure. In early 2004, he concluded—along with FBI Director Robert Mueller, Deputy Attorney General James Comey, and Attorney General John Ashcroft—that the NSA spying program violated FISA, which requires judicial approval for electronic surveillance of US citizens and permanent residents. And in June 2004, he withdrew the Justice Department's infamous August 2002 memo on torture, drafted by John Yoo at Alberto Gonzales's request. This memo, in effect, allowed the CIA to use harsh interrogation tactics, including waterboarding, head-slapping, sleep deprivation, stress positions, and exposure to extremes of heat and cold, by assuring CIA agents that they would not be prosecuted for violating the federal torture statute. Goldsmith writes:

> The message of the August 1, 2002, OLC opinion was indeed clear: violent acts aren't necessarily torture; if you do torture, you probably have a defense; and even if you don't have a defense, the torture law doesn't apply if you act under color of presidential authority. CIA interrogators and their supervisors, under pressure to get information about the next attack, viewed the opinion as a "golden shield," as one CIA official later called it, that provided enormous comfort.

Goldsmith did not come to these positions lightly. In his view, the OLC should approve presidential action so long as there is any reasonable legal argument available to defend it. In these instances, he apparently concluded that no reasonable lawyer could say "yes." Or, in other words, David Addington and John Yoo were not reasonable lawyers.

Goldsmith has received widespread and deserved commendation for his courage in standing up against these assertions of unchecked executive power, at both personal and professional cost.[5] John Yoo, once a close friend, no longer speaks to him. And saying "no" was not a way to get ahead in the Bush administration. Patrick Philbin, who worked with Goldsmith at the OLC and reportedly supported Goldsmith's challenges to the White House, was vetoed for a prestigious post in the solicitor general's office for having done so.

Still, when one probes more deeply, Goldsmith's differences with Addington often turn out to be more about style and prudence than about substance. Goldsmith rarely criticizes any of the administration's policies on their merits, whether the CIA's interrogation tactics

---

5. See, for example, Jeffrey Rosen, "Conscience of a Conservative," *The New York Times Magazine*, September 9, 2007.

or disappearances into secret prisons or detentions at Guantánamo or military tribunals. His complaint is not that these measures were wrong, but simply that it would have been more diplomatic to seek congressional authorization for them. Thus he cites with approval the 2006 Military Commissions Act (MCA), which stripped Guantánamo detainees of habeas corpus review, authorized the admission of coerced testimony in military trials, retroactively immunized CIA interrogators from prosecution for war crimes, barred foreign nationals from invoking the Geneva Conventions in court, and watered down the federal war crimes statute. Goldsmith takes issue with none of these developments, and instead praises the MCA as "an important first step in the right direction of putting counterterrorism policy on a more secure and sensible legal foundation."

Similarly, while Goldsmith differed with the White House over the NSA spying program during the spring of 2004, he ultimately approved a program that appears to have violated criminal law. Goldsmith initially sided with Comey, Mueller, and Ashcroft in concluding that some aspects of the program as it existed in 2004 were illegal. This is what led to the now-famous March 2004 hospital room confrontation, in which White House Counsel Alberto Gonzales sought to get an ailing and sedated Ashcroft to reverse his own prior decision and approve the NSA program.[6] Thanks to candid congressional testimony from Comey, it will not be difficult to stage the scene for the inevitable made-for-television movie. In an interview with Jeffrey Rosen for a *New York Times Magazine* article, Goldsmith added the detail that Mrs. Ashcroft stuck her tongue out at Gonzales and White House Chief of Staff Andrew Card as they left the room, having been rebuffed by Ashcroft from his sick bed.

But we still do not know what aspect of the program prompted the disagreement—and Goldsmith does not tell us. What we do know is

---

6. I recount the story of that confrontation in Chapter One, "The Fundamentalist and the Facilitator," pp. 4–6.

that once the White House agreed to change the program, Goldsmith and others fell into line and approved it, despite its apparent continuing illegality. The Justice Department's legal opinion defending that altered program, which Goldsmith presumably approved and which has now been made public, authorizes warrantless wiretapping of Americans' international calls to or from persons suspected of ties to al-Qaeda, and does so by relying heavily on the Addington-Cheney view that the president has uncheckable constitutional authority to ignore criminal statutes when engaging the enemy in wartime.[7]

While Goldsmith reserves his harshest criticism for the August 2002 torture memo, that is an easy target, and he appears to have taken no steps to halt any of the interrogation tactics it authorized. The memo infamously maintained that torture was limited to the infliction of physical pain at a level associated with organ failure or death, thus permitting all lesser forms of physical abuse. Goldsmith writes that no one in the administration other than Addington was willing to defend the memo once it became public. In his recent confirmation hearing for the post of attorney general, Judge Michael Mukasey called the August 2002 memo "worse than a sin." To Goldsmith's credit, he recognized that it was deeply flawed before the photographs from Abu Ghraib were released, and before the memo was leaked to the press. But it is telling that he did not actually withdraw it until after the memo was leaked.

More disturbing, while Goldsmith ultimately withdrew the memo, he did not succeed in issuing a replacement: the new memo was drafted in December 2004 by his successor, Daniel Levin, after Goldsmith had resigned. Most disturbing of all, even after Goldsmith withdrew the August 2002 memo, he never requested that a single interrogation tactic previously approved on the basis of the retracted

---

7. For a critique of these arguments, see the appendix, "On NSA Spying: A Letter to Congress."

memo be prohibited. In his book, he says only that he "just didn't yet know" whether any of the CIA methods were illegal, an evasion remarkably similar to Judge Mukasey's recent statements that he is unable to say whether waterboarding is torture. Goldsmith's failure to reach a decision meant that the CIA continued to engage in waterboarding, head slapping, stress positions, sleep deprivation, and the like, even after the August 2002 memo was withdrawn. And while Goldsmith harshly criticizes the Yoo memo, his objections are that it was "wildly broader than was necessary," "tendentious [in] tone," and lacked "care and sobriety." In other words, to Goldsmith the memo's sin was that it was poorly drafted, not that the tactics it authorized were illegal and immoral and had to be stopped.

In fact, in discussing the December 2004 memo drafted by Levin, Goldsmith cites with approval a footnote stating that "we have reviewed this Office's prior opinions addressing issues involving treatment of detainees and do not believe that any of their conclusions would be different under the standards set forth in this memorandum." Goldsmith cites this footnote as evidence that the August 2002 memo was unnecessarily broad, which it certainly was. But he expresses no concern that even after the initial memo was replaced, waterboarding and other forms of torture continued to be used and approved.

For all its strengths as a descriptive account of an administration run amok, the prescriptive elements of *The Terror Presidency* are at best conventional and at worst perverse. Holding up Franklin Delano Roosevelt as a model, Goldsmith recommends that the executive branch should take a more diplomatic approach to the other branches of government. As a matter of realpolitik, he suggests, the executive might well consolidate and exercise its power more effectively by working with Congress and the courts than by aggressively asserting immunity from legislative and judicial oversight on national security matters. What is striking is not the content of this prescription, which in itself is neither novel nor controversial, but the fact that Addington and other members of the Bush administration so vehemently rejected it.

The most provocative aspect of Goldsmith's argument, however, is also the least persuasive. He contends that the problem was not that Addington and the administration did not care sufficiently about the law, but that they cared too intensely, so much so that they were "strangled by law." He claims that "this war has been lawyered to death," and describes government officials as overly chilled by the prospect that they might be held criminally accountable for actions taken in the name of the country's security. Goldsmith prefers the good old days when matters of national security and war were, for the most part, not regulated by federal legislation, and presidents, such as FDR, were free to shape their judgments without regard for law, and could concentrate instead on "political legitimation." In the post-Watergate era, he laments, Congress passed "many of the laws that so infuriatingly tied the President's hands in the post-9/11 world." This view, of course, is fully consonant with that of Cheney and Addington. Cheney, for example, told reporters on board Air Force One in 2005 that "a lot of the things around Watergate and Vietnam both, in the seventies, served to erode the authority I think the President needs."

What exactly are the laws that Goldsmith thinks "so infuriatingly tied the President's hands?" The only ones that he discusses are the War Crimes Act, which makes some Geneva Convention violations a federal crime; the federal torture statute, which makes torture inflicted abroad a felony; and the Foreign Intelligence Surveillance Act, which requires judicial approval of wiretapping targeted at US citizens and permanent residents. Which of these laws would Goldsmith do away with? He does not say. And does he really think that Addington, Gonzales, Cheney, and Bush would have acted more prudently if there had been no laws barring torture, warrantless wiretapping, and crimes of war? The only reason these officials had to listen to Goldsmith at all was that there were laws in place that limited their options. And the limits themselves are not especially onerous. FISA does not forbid surveillance, but merely requires judicial oversight. The torture statute does not preclude interrogation, but prohibits only torture. And the War Crimes Act merely enforces the very laws of war that we insisted on enforcing against the Nazis after World War II.

It is true that FDR was not subject to these laws. But Goldsmith never identifies any causal connection between the absence of formal legal restraints and FDR's willingness to collaborate with Congress. It is highly implausible that Bush and Cheney would have been more open to diplomacy had they faced fewer restraints. What restraints they faced they sought to avoid through subterfuge and legal gamesmanship—redefining torture so that it could be used, issuing "signing statements" that asserted the power to ignore the very laws the president was officially approving, and claiming in secret that other laws simply did not apply to actions that they were clearly intended to cover. Those taking the "push, push, push" attitude would have reveled in the absence of legal restraints, because then there would have been no "larger force" to make them stop.

Goldsmith writes convincingly that the pressures on an administration fearful of another terrorist attack are so strong that the executive feels obligated to do everything it can to stop the next attack. He contends that "this is why the question 'What should we do?' so often collapsed into the question 'What can we lawfully do?'" But if his account of this pressure is accurate, it only underscores the need for legal restraints. Indeed, it is because of the abuse of executive power in times of crisis that we now have laws regulating torture, the treatment of enemy detainees, and wiretapping for foreign intelligence.

Ironically, had the laws Goldsmith condemns as "paralyzing" not been on the books, he would have had no standing to resist Addington's relentless drive to expand executive power. The laws governing warfare, interrogation, and surveillance were written to rein in such people as Addington, and their ultimate effectiveness turns on having people like Goldsmith and Comey in office willing to enforce them. If Goldsmith's perverse proposal to erase the very lines he drew were accepted, the result would be disastrous for future efforts to restrain rampant executive power.

4

WHY THE COURT SAID NO

SINCE THE FIRST FEW DAYS after the terrorist attacks of September 11, 2001, the Bush administration has taken the view that the president has unilateral, unchecked authority to wage a war, not only against those who attacked us on that day, but against all terrorist organizations of potentially global reach. The administration claims that the president's role as commander in chief of the armed forces grants him exclusive authority to select "the means and methods of engaging the enemy."[1] And it has interpreted that power in turn to permit President Bush to take actions that Congress made illegal.

In advocating these positions, which I will collectively call "the Bush doctrine," the administration has brushed aside legal objections as mere hindrances to the ultimate goal of keeping Americans safe. It has argued that domestic criminal and constitutional law are of little concern because the president's powers as commander in chief override all such laws; that the Geneva Conventions, a set of international treaties that regulate the treatment of prisoners during war, simply do not apply to the conflict with al-Qaeda; and more broadly still, that the president

---

1. Department of Justice, "Legal Authorities Supporting the Activities of the National Security Agency Described by the President" (January 19, 2006), available at www.cdt.org/security/nsa/20060116doj.pdf.

has unilateral authority to defy international law. In short, there is little to distinguish the current administration's view from that famously espoused by President Richard Nixon when asked to justify his authorization of illegal, warrantless wiretapping of Americans during the Vietnam War: "When the president does it, that means that it is not illegal."

If another nation's leader adopted such positions, the United States would be quick to condemn him or her for violating fundamental tenets of the rule of law, human rights, and the separation of powers. But President Bush has largely gotten away with it, at least at home, for at least three reasons. Until 2006, his party held a decisive majority in Congress, making effective political checks by that branch highly unlikely. Even when it took control of Congress, the Democratic Party largely shied away from directly challenging the president for fear that it would be viewed as soft on terrorism. And the American public has for the most part offered only muted objections.

These realities make the Supreme Court's decision in *Hamdan* v. *Rumsfeld*, issued on the last day of its 2005–2006 term, in equal parts stunning and crucial. Stunning because the Court, unlike Congress, the opposition party, or the American people, actually stood up to the president. Crucial because the Court's decision, while on the surface narrowly focused on whether the military tribunals President Bush created to try foreign suspects for war crimes were consistent with US law, marked, at a deeper level, a dramatic refutation of the administration's entire approach to the "war on terror."

At bottom, the *Hamdan* case stands for the proposition that the rule of law—including international law—is not subservient to the will of the executive, even during wartime. As Justice John Paul Stevens wrote in the concluding lines of his opinion for the majority:

> In undertaking to try Hamdan and subject him to criminal punishment, the Executive is bound to comply with the Rule of Law that prevails in this jurisdiction.

The notion that government must abide by law is hardly radical. Its implications for the "war on terror" are radical, however, precisely because the Bush doctrine has so fundamentally challenged that very idea.

Salim Hamdan, a citizen of Yemen, has been held at Guantánamo Bay since June 2002. At the time of the Supreme Court's decision, he was one of only fourteen men at Guantánamo who had been designated by the administration to be tried for war crimes—the remaining 440 or so had never been charged with any criminal conduct. Hamdan was charged with conspiracy to commit war crimes by serving as Osama bin Laden's driver and bodyguard, and by attending an al-Qaeda training camp.

The tribunal set up to try Hamdan was created by an executive order issued in November 2001. Its rules were draconian. They permitted defendants to be tried and convicted on the basis of evidence that neither they nor their chosen civilian lawyers had any chance to see or rebut. They allowed the use of hearsay evidence, which similarly deprives the defendant of an opportunity to cross-examine his accuser. They excluded information obtained by torture, but permitted testimony coerced by any means short of torture. They denied the defendant the right to be present at all phases of his own trial. They empowered the secretary of defense or his subordinate to intervene in the trial and decide central issues in the case instead of the presiding judge. And finally, the rules were predicated on a double standard, since these procedures applied only to foreign nationals accused of acts of terrorism, not US citizens.

Hamdan's lawyers challenged the legality of the military tribunals in federal court before his trial had even begun, arguing that the president lacked authority to create the tribunals in the first place, and that the tribunals' structure and procedures violated the Constitution, US military law, and the Geneva Conventions.

To say that Hamdan faced an uphill battle is a gross understatement. The Supreme Court has said in the past that foreign nationals who are outside US borders, like Hamdan, lack any constitutional protections. Hamdan was a member of the enemy forces when he was captured, and courts are especially reluctant to interfere with the military's treatment of "enemy aliens" in wartime. He filed his suit before trial, and courts generally prefer to wait until a trial is completed before assessing its legality. And as recently as World War II, the Supreme Court upheld the use of military tribunals, and ruled that the Geneva Conventions are not enforceable by individuals in US courts but may be enforced only through diplomatic means.

Surprisingly, Hamdan prevailed in the district court, when US District Judge James Robertson courageously ruled that trying Hamdan in a military tribunal of the kind set up by the government would violate the Geneva Conventions. Not surprisingly, that decision was unanimously reversed, on every conceivable ground, by the Court of Appeals for the D.C. Circuit, in an opinion joined fully by then Judge, now Chief Justice, John Roberts. And as if Hamdan did not face enough hurdles, after the Supreme Court agreed to hear his case, Congress passed a law that appeared to be designed to strip the Supreme Court of its jurisdiction to hear the case. The Detainee Treatment Act of 2005 required defendants in military tribunals to undergo their trials before seeking judicial review, and prescribed the D.C. Circuit as the exclusive forum for such review.

In its arguments to the Supreme Court, the administration invoked the Bush doctrine. It argued that the president has "inherent authority to convene military commissions to try and punish captured enemy combatants in wartime," even without congressional authorization, and that therefore the Court should be extremely hesitant to find that Bush's actions violated the law.[2] And it insisted that in

---

2. Brief for Respondents in *Hamdan* v. *Rumsfeld*, p. 8.

declaring that the Geneva Conventions did not apply to al-Qaeda Bush had exercised his constitutional war powers, and his decision was therefore "binding on the courts."[3]

The Supreme Court, by a vote of 5–3, rejected the president's contentions. (Chief Justice Roberts did not participate, since it was his own decision that was under review.) The Court's principal opinion was written by its senior justice, John Paul Stevens, a World War II veteran, and the only justice who has served in the military. He was joined in full by Justices Ginsburg, Souter, and Breyer, and in the main by Justice Kennedy. Kennedy also wrote a separate concurring opinion, and because he provided the crucial fifth vote, his views may prove more significant in the long run.[4]

The Court found, first, that the administration's procedures for military tribunals deviated significantly from the court-martial procedures used to try members of our own armed forces, and that the Uniform Code of Military Justice barred such deviations unless it could be shown that court-martial procedures would be "impracticable." The administration made no such showing, the Court observed, and therefore the tribunals violated the limit set by Congress in the Uniform Code. The Court could well have stopped there. This conclusion was a fully sufficient rationale to rule for Hamdan and invalidate the tribunals. Had it done so, the decision would have been far less consequential, since Congress could easily have changed its law or declared that court-martial procedures are impracticable.

But the Court went on to find that Congress had also required military tribunals to conform to the law of war, and that the tribunals

---

3. Brief for Respondents in *Hamdan*, p. 38.

4. Because only eight justices participated, Kennedy's vote was crucial in the sense that had he sided with the dissenters, the Court would have divided evenly, 4–4, which would have had the legal effect of affirming the Circuit Court's decision. In future cases involving military tribunals, Chief Justice Roberts will participate and likely side with the dissenters, and in that event Justice Kennedy's vote will again be decisive.

use of military tribunals. And it ruled that whatever inherent power the president might have in the absence of congressional legislation, "he may not disregard limitations that Congress has, in proper exercise of its own war powers, placed on his powers."

These conclusions squarely refute the only arguments President Bush has advanced to justify the NSA spying program. The AUMF of 2001 is as silent on wiretapping as it is on military tribunals. Here too, then, the president may not disregard Congress's express limitations on his powers.

The most far-reaching implications of the Court's decision, however, concern the interrogation of al-Qaeda suspects. The administration has since the outset of the conflict sought to evade the limitations set by international law on coercive interrogation, reasoning that the need for "actionable intelligence" trumps the human dignity of its detainees.[6] According to a January 25, 2002, memo from then White House counsel Alberto Gonzales to the president, the desire to extract information from suspects was a prime motivating factor behind the administration's decision that the Geneva Conventions do not apply to the conflict with al-Qaeda. The Justice Department's infamous "torture memo" of August 2002 argued, among other things, that threatening death and inflicting pain short of death or organ failure were not "torture," and that in any event the president as commander in chief could order torture despite a criminal statute prohibiting it.

The administration also secretly interpreted the International Convention Against Torture and Other Cruel, Inhuman and Degrading Treatment, ratified by Congress in 1994, to *permit* cruel and degrading treatment of foreign nationals held outside US borders. When

---

6. See Mark Danner, *Torture and Truth: America, Abu Ghraib, and the War on Terror* (New York Review Books, 2004).

Senator John McCain convinced Congress to overrule that interpretation by statute, the administration lobbied members of Congress to ensure that the McCain Amendment contained no enforceable sanctions. It then attached a "signing statement" to the law proclaiming that the president would obey the amendment only to the extent that it did not interfere with his decisions as commander in chief—in other words, only when he chose to obey it.

The *Hamdan* decision, while not explicitly addressed to the question of interrogation, went a long way toward resolving this debate. Common Article 3 of the Geneva Conventions, which the Court has now authoritatively declared applies to the conflict with al-Qaeda, requires that all detainees be "treated humanely," and protects them against "outrages upon personal dignity, in particular humiliating and degrading treatment." Thus, CIA and military interrogators are now on notice that any inhumane treatment of a detainee violates the laws of war. While they might be confident that the Bush administration would not prosecute them, they cannot be sure that a future administration would overlook such acts. And it is quite possible that government officials might actually decide not to violate the law—now that they know such action is illegal—even if prosecution is unlikely.

On July 11, 2006, the administration announced that Deputy Secretary of Defense Gordon England had issued a memo to military officers instructing them that the Supreme Court had ruled that Common Article 3 applies to the conflict with al-Qaeda, and ordering them to ensure that their practices conformed to Common Article 3. Some news accounts characterized this as a "major policy shift," but in fact the memo merely stated what the Supreme Court decided. The memo did suggest that the military had always been abiding by a directive from President Bush to treat detainees "humanely." What it did not say, however, is that administration lawyers had claimed under that dictate that the following tactics were legally available for interrogating al-Qaeda suspects: forced nudity; "using detainees[']

individual phobias (such as fear of dogs) to induce stress"; water-boarding; and "scenarios designed to convince the detainee that death or severely painful consequences are imminent for him and/or his family." In addition, the military found nothing inhumane about the interrogation of a Guantánamo detainee that included forcing him to strip naked and wear women's underwear, putting him on a leash and making him bark like a dog, and injecting him with intravenous fluids and then barring him from going to the bathroom, forcing him to uri-nate on himself. If the military considers all of this "humane," the assertion that it will abide by Common Article 3 is meaningless.

In the Military Commissions Act, Congress sought to soften the impact of the *Hamdan* decision on interrogation practices by simulta-neously extending retroactive immunity to CIA officials who had used coercive tactics in the past, and limiting the definition of "war crimes" under US law to specified "grave breaches" of Common Arti-cle 3, excluding from domestic prosecution those who merely treat detainees inhumanely. But a violation of Common Article 3 remains a violation of the international law of war. Surely the last message we should want to send to the rest of the world is that the McCain Amendment's ban on all cruel, inhuman, and degrading treatment was only for show, because we are not actually willing to be bound by such a ban if it has any enforceable effect.

In fact, the Court's decision further suggests that President Bush has *already* committed a war crime, by establishing the military tri-bunals and subjecting detainees to them. As noted above, the Court found that the tribunals violated Common Article 3, and under the War Crimes Act prior to its amendment by the Military Commissions Act, any violation of Common Article 3 was a war crime. Military defense lawyers responded to the *Hamdan* decision by requesting a stay of all tribunal proceedings, on the ground that their own contin-uing participation in those proceedings might constitute a war crime. According to the logic of the Supreme Court, President Bush had already committed a war crime. He won't be prosecuted, of course, and probably should not be, since his interpretation of the conventions was at least arguable. But now his interpretation has been conclusively rejected, so both the ongoing tribunals and our interrogation rules must conform to Article 3's requirements.

Some have argued that the Court's decision in *Hamdan* was too timid, because it rested on statutory rather than on constitutional grounds, and thereby left the door open for Congress to undercut the Court's decision through legislation, as Congress then did in the Military Commissions Act. But in choosing to decide the case despite Congress's apparent attempt to divest the Court of jurisdiction, in holding that the president is bound by congressional limitations even when acting as commander in chief, and most importantly in declaring that Common Article 3 governs the conflict with al-Qaeda, the Court's decision was anything but restrained. It was a potent refutation of the Bush doctrine, and a much-needed resurrection of the rule of law.

This lesson is especially clear when *Hamdan* is read in conjunction with the Court's decisions two years earlier in the "enemy combatant" cases. In those cases, also clear defeats for the president, the Court rejected the administration's arguments that prisoners at Guantánamo had no right of access to federal courts to challenge the legality of their detention, and that US citizens held as "enemy combatants" had no right to a hearing to challenge whether they were in fact "enemy combatants." The administration's lawyers had put forward the Bush doctrine there, too, arguing that it would be unconstitutional for Congress or the courts to interfere with the president's unilateral power as commander in chief to detain the enemy. But the Court rejected that view, insisting that

> whatever power the United States Constitution envisions for the Executive in its exchanges with other nations or with enemy

organizations in times of conflict, it most assuredly envisions a role for all three branches when individual liberties are at stake.[7]

The *Hamdan* decision confirms not only that all three branches have a role to play, but that international law itself has an essential role, in particular the laws of war that the administration has for so long sought to evade. The significance of the decision is perhaps best captured by the reaction of two of the Bush doctrine's principal architects. John Yoo, the former Justice Department lawyer who wrote the torture memo, objected that "what the court is doing is attempting to suppress creative thinking.... It could affect every aspect of the war on terror." And Bradford Berenson, associate White House counsel from 2001 to 2003, lamented that "what is truly radical is the Supreme Court's willingness to bend to world opinion."

If by "creative thinking" Yoo means torturing suspects, "disappearing" them into CIA black sites, holding them indefinitely without hearings, and trying them in tribunals that permit people to be executed on the basis of secret evidence, then perhaps creative thinking should be suppressed. Bending to world opinion would indeed be a radical change for a president who, during the 2004 presidential debates, derisively rejected concern with how the United States is seen around the world as an unacceptable "global test." But making US practice conform to the international rules that formally reflect world opinion is a necessary first step if we are to begin to reduce the unprecedented levels of anti-American sentiment found among our allies and foes alike, and offset the propaganda advantage our unilateral approach has given to al-Qaeda.

The Bush doctrine views the rule of law as our enemy. In fact, the security of the nation in the struggle with terrorists rests on adherence to the rule of law, including international law, because only such

---

7. *Hamdi v. Rumsfeld*, 542 U.S. 507 (2004).

adherence provides the legitimacy we need if we are to win back the world's respect. *Hamdan* suggests that at least one branch of the United States government understands this.

5

UNCLE SAM IS WATCHING YOU

IN OCTOBER 2003, CONGRESS VOTED to end Total Information Awareness (TIA), a Pentagon plan designed to analyze vast amounts of computer data about all of us in order to search for patterns of terrorist activity. At the time, the vote in Congress seemed one of the most notable victories for privacy since September 11. Computers record virtually everything we do these days—whom we call or e-mail, what books and magazines we read, what Web sites we search, where we travel, which videos we rent, and everything we buy by credit card or check. The prospect of the military and security agencies constantly trolling through all of this information about innocent citizens in hopes of finding terrorists led Congress to ban spending on the program.

Admittedly, much of the credit for TIA's defeat has to go to the Pentagon's public relations department, which not only gave the program its less than reassuring name, but also came up with a logo consisting of a pyramid topped by a large, digitized eye and the Latin motto *Scientia Est Potentia*, or "Knowledge Is Power." George Orwell and Michel Foucault could hardly have done better. It also helped that the Pentagon's Defense Advanced Research Projects Agency (DARPA), which developed the plan, was headed by John Poindexter, who had been convicted of lying to Congress in the Iran-contra affair, and whose conviction had been overturned on appeal only on a technicality. The vote to kill TIA came shortly after DARPA floated the idea of creating a market for betting on terrorist attacks and other disasters. Still, the fact that Congress rejected TIA seemed to suggest that it was willing to stand up for privacy even in the face of the threat of catastrophic terrorism.

But reports of the death of TIA were greatly exaggerated. Federal programs to collect and search vast computer databases for security purposes continue virtually unabated, inside and outside the Pentagon. The congressional ban did not apply to the Pentagon's classified budget, so the military's development of programs to collect and analyze computer data has simply moved behind closed doors. Congress has directed the Department of Homeland Security to develop "data mining and other advanced analytic tools... to access, receive and analyze data, detect and identify threats of terrorism against the United States." And with federal funding, several states are cooperating in the Multistate Antiterrorism Regional Information Exchange System, or MATRIX, which links law enforcement records with other government and private databases in order to identify suspected terrorists.

The private firm that is running MATRIX, Sesint, based in Florida, previously compiled a "terrorist index" of 120,000 persons using

> such factors as age, gender, ethnicity, credit history, "investigational data," information about pilot and driver licenses, and connections to "dirty" addresses known to have been used by other suspects.

Thus, despite the apparent victory for civil libertarians in stopping TIA itself, data mining remains a central instrument in the government's response to the threat of terrorism. As a special committee appointed by Defense Secretary Donald Rumsfeld wrote in its recently released report, "TIA was not the tip of the iceberg, but rather one small specimen in a sea of icebergs."

Data mining, the computerized analysis of extensive electronic databases about private individuals for patterns of suspicious activity, is just one example of the threats to privacy that Americans have faced following the terrorist attacks of September 11, 2001. Since then, through the USA Patriot Act and various executive initiatives, the government has authorized official monitoring of attorney–client conversations, wide-ranging secret searches and wiretaps, the collection of Internet and e-mail addressing data, spying on religious services and the meetings of political groups, and the collection of library and other business records. All this can be done without first showing probable cause that the people being investigated are engaged in criminal activity, the usual threshold that must be passed before the government may invade privacy.

Of course, these laws and policies merely authorize such snooping. They do not compel it. The administration's message since September 11 has been "trust us." President Bush and Vice President Dick Cheney say that critics have cited "no abuses" of the USA Patriot Act, as if to suggest that absence of visible abuse shows that we can trust them. But the "no abuses" defense is fundamentally misleading in two respects.

First, there have in fact been abuses of the Patriot Act. In June 2004, a jury in Idaho acquitted Sami Omar al-Hussayen, an Idaho student charged under the Patriot Act for aiding terrorism because he had a Web site that included links to other Web sites that included some speeches endorsing terrorism. The government never even alleged, much less proved, that al-Hussayen had intended to further any terrorist activity. Under its theory, any posting of a link to a Web site advocating terrorism is a violation of the Patriot Act's ban on providing "expert advice and assistance" to designated "terrorist organizations." If that's true, *The New York Times* could be prosecuted for including a link to Osama bin Laden's latest recorded message, and it would be no defense to show that the link was posted solely for educational purposes.

In another case involving the same Patriot Act provision, the Humanitarian Law Project, a human rights group in Los Angeles, faces the threat of criminal prosecution for advising a Kurdish group in Turkey on protecting human rights. The project has provided the training precisely to discourage violence and to encourage the pursuit of lawful means to advance Kurdish rights in Turkey. Yet the administration claims that it can prosecute such human rights advocacy as "material support of terrorism," even though it consists solely of speech and is not intended to promote violence. The courts have thus far ruled that the Patriot Act's application to such activity is unconstitutional, but the Bush administration is appealing.

Similarly ominous is the case of Khader Hamide and Michel Shehadeh, two longstanding permanent resident aliens from Palestine now in Los Angeles.[1] They have lived in the US for more than twenty-five and thirty years, respectively, and have never been charged with a crime. The administration tried to deport them under the Patriot Act for having distributed magazines of a PLO faction in Los Angeles during the 1980s. The government did not dispute that it was entirely lawful to distribute the magazines at the time, or that the magazines are themselves legal and available in libraries across the country. Yet it claimed that under the Patriot Act, it could retroactively deport the two Palestinians for engaging in activity that would plainly be protected by the First Amendment if engaged in by US citizens. In October 2007, after an immigration judge dismissed the deportation case for prosecutorial misconduct, the administration agreed to abandon its deportation effort.

Still another provision of the Patriot Act allows the government to freeze the assets of any person or entity it chooses, simply by claiming that he or it is under "investigation." It can then defend the action in court with secret evidence, presented to the court in a closed session

---

1. I represent both men as well as the Humanitarian Law Project, mentioned above.

but not disclosed to the entity or person whose assets have been frozen. The Bush administration has used this authority to close down several leading Muslim charities in the United States, without ever having to prove that they actually financed terrorism, and without affording the charities an opportunity to defend themselves.

In July 2004, the administration invoked the Patriot Act to deny entry to Tariq Ramadan, a highly respected Swiss-born Muslim scholar. Ramadan, a moderate hired by Notre Dame to fill a chair in international peace studies, was apparently excluded under a Patriot Act ban on those who "endorse terrorism." The administration has refused to specify his allegedly offending words.

And in September 2004, a federal court in New York ruled that the FBI's enforcement of still another Patriot Act provision squarely violated the First and Fourth Amendments. The court ruled that the provision, which authorizes the FBI to compel Internet service providers to turn over information about their customers, is invalid because it prohibits the provider from disclosing to anyone—even a lawyer—that the FBI request was made, and effectively precludes any judicial review.

So the first problem with the administration's claim that there have been no abuses under the Patriot Act is that it is simply false. There have been plenty of abuses.

The second problem is more insidious. Many of the Patriot Act's most controversial provisions involve investigative powers that are by definition secret, making it literally impossible for abuses to be uncovered. For example, the act expanded the authority to conduct wiretaps and searches under the Foreign Intelligence Surveillance Act (FISA) without having to show probable cause of criminal activity. We know from a government report that the number of FISA searches has dramatically increased since the Patriot Act was passed, and for the first time now exceeds the number of conventional wiretaps authorized in criminal cases. Yet that's all we know, because everything else about FISA searches and wiretaps is secret.

The target of a FISA search is never notified, unless evidence from the search is subsequently used in a criminal prosecution, and even then the defendant cannot see the application for the search, and therefore cannot test its legality in court. When the attorney general uses conventional criminal wiretaps, he is required to file an extensive report listing the legal basis for each wiretap, its duration, and whether it resulted in a criminal charge or conviction. But no such information is required under FISA. The annual report detailing use of the criminal wiretap authority exceeds one hundred pages; the report on the use of FISA is a one-page letter.

Another provision of the Patriot Act radically expands the government's ability to obtain personal business records without showing probable cause. Before the Patriot Act was passed, the government had to limit its inquiries to a specific set of financial, phone, and travel records, and these could be obtained only if the target was an "agent of a foreign power." The Patriot Act expanded the definition of records that may be seized, so that it now includes, among other things, library and bookstore records and medical files. And it eliminated the requirement that the person whose records are sought be an "agent of a foreign power." Now the government can get anyone's records. Here, too, the authority is veiled in secrecy. The Patriot Act makes it a crime for the person or organization ordered to produce records to tell anyone about the request. The act does not require the government to notify people whose records have been reviewed, and does not require that any report of its activities be made available to the public.

The Internet service provider that brought the successful challenge to the Patriot Act described above had to violate the law's nondisclosure provision to do so, and the lawsuit itself had to be filed in secret until the court allowed its existence to be acknowledged.

The administration's challenge to critics to come forward with examples of abuse under the Patriot Act was therefore disingenuous. The most controversial provisions contain legal requirements of secrecy

searches and seizures.[3] His book presents a tale of two courts—the Warren Court of the 1950s and 1960s, which aggressively expanded the protection of privacy, and today's Rehnquist Court, which has just as aggressively decimated those rights. Like the great lawyer he was, Dash uses his stories to argue persuasively for the resurrection of meaningful judicial safeguards.

The Naked Crowd, by Jeffrey Rosen, a professor at George Washington University School of Law, considers the political, financial, and psychological factors that are likely to shape the law of privacy in the decades to come.[4] Rosen spends less time on the law as such, and more on the social forces at play in the Internet age; our privacy, he argues, is threatened not only by government programs like TIA but by the public's low estimate of the value of privacy. Rosen is skeptical about the courts' willingness to protect privacy, but guardedly optimistic about Congress's ability to do so.

In his book, Dash reminds us that real safeguards against official intrusion into the lives and affairs of the people took centuries to develop. He notes, for example, that the Magna Carta did not bar the king from searching private homes whenever he wanted. And until 1961 the US Constitution's protections against unreasonable searches and seizures did not extend to state and local police, who carry out over 90 percent of law enforcement. In that year, the Supreme Court first applied the "exclusionary rule" to the states, meaning that evidence obtained in violation of the Fourth Amendment had to be excluded from the case against a defendant. Similarly, the Court did not give indigent defendants the right to appointed lawyers until 1963, and did not create Miranda rights in police interrogations until 1966.

---

3. Samuel Dash, *The Intruders: Unreasonable Searches and Seizures from King John to John Ashcroft* (Rutgers University Press, 2004).

4. *The Naked Crowd: Reclaiming Security and Freedom in an Anxious Age* (Random House, 2004).

There are good reasons why the rights of privacy and liberty flourished in the civil rights era. That period, perhaps more than any other, demonstrated the danger of unconstrained law enforcement, as Southern police and the FBI alike harassed and prosecuted civil rights activists, using the criminal law as a means to monitor, regulate, and penalize dissent.

Dash demonstrates, however, that almost as soon as the Fourth Amendment was extended to the states, the Supreme Court under Chief Justices Burger and Rehnquist began whittling away its protections. The Court created many exceptions to the "exclusionary rule" in the 1970s, permitting illegally obtained evidence to be used, for example, in grand jury, immigration, and civil tax proceedings. In 1978, the Court allowed the government to use illegally obtained evidence to incriminate anyone other than the person whose privacy rights were violated. In 1984, it ruled that as long as the police obtained a search warrant, the exclusionary rule ought not apply, even if the warrant itself was illegal. These exceptions dramatically weakened Fourth Amendment protections by telling police that they can use illegally obtained evidence for a wide variety of purposes.

The Court under Burger and Rehnquist also directly relaxed the requirements of the Fourth Amendment, allowing a great many kinds of searches without warrants or probable cause at all. Most of these changes were made in the context of the "war on drugs." Because narcotics are easy to conceal and there are often no complaining witnesses to drug crimes, the usual requirement that the police show probable cause that a person possesses an illegal substance before they can search him posed a considerable obstacle to enforcing drug laws. The Court accordingly relaxed the Constitution's requirements. But if the Fourth Amendment could not withstand the pressures of the war on drugs, how is it likely to fare in the war on terrorism?

Both Rosen and Dash express particular concern about data mining, which they compare to the "general warrants" that allowed the

British colonial government to search anyone's home, without having any prior ground for suspicion. Like "general warrants," data mining permits officials to search the private computer records of innocent people without any specific basis of suspicion. Objections to "general warrants" inspired the Fourth Amendment; yet the Framers could not have contemplated computerized searches of extensive public and private databases. And therefore, Dash suggests, it is up to the Supreme Court to extend Fourth Amendment principles to modern practices.

Ironically, the Supreme Court decision that is widely credited with adapting the Fourth Amendment to the twentieth century now threatens to render it powerless to regulate data mining and other modern surveillance techniques in the twenty-first. In its 1967 decision *Katz v. United States,* the Supreme Court reversed forty years of precedent and ruled that the Fourth Amendment's prohibition on unreasonable searches and seizures applies to electronic eavesdropping and wiretapping. Federal officials had placed a listening device on a phone booth used by Charles Katz and had overheard him discussing illegal gambling activities. They did not obtain a warrant, because in previous decisions, the Supreme Court had ruled that the Fourth Amendment was not implicated so long as the government's investigatory tactics did not invade a person's property. Since Katz had no "property interest" in the phone booth, the federal government reasoned, there was no need to obtain a warrant to listen in on his phone call.

The Court in the *Katz* case held that the Fourth Amendment "protects people, not places." Under the new approach, the Fourth Amendment is violated whenever the police invade an individual's "reasonable expectation of privacy," regardless of property rights. Since people reasonably expect their phone conversations to be private, the police cannot listen in without a warrant and probable cause.

The *Katz* decision has long been hailed for recognizing the need to adapt the Fourth Amendment to advances in technology. Once phones could be tapped without going anywhere near a caller's property, the Court's property-based approach no longer made sense. Nothing less than a major shift in Fourth Amendment jurisprudence was required, and *Katz* provided it.

Today, however, a second and equally momentous shift is needed. The development of computer technologies threatens to radically alter the balance between privacy and security. Computers make it possible to find, store, exchange, retrieve, and analyze vast amounts of information about our private lives in ways that previously were unthinkable. But while the Court's ruling in *Katz* freed Fourth Amendment doctrine from its moorings in antiquated notions of property, its emphasis on "reasonable expectations of privacy" left privacy vulnerable to future advances in technology. As technology makes it increasingly easy to invade spaces that used to be private through the use of enhanced listening, viewing, and other sensing devices, "expectations of privacy" and the protection of the Fourth Amendment may be radically reduced.

The Rehnquist Court's most disturbing application of the *Katz* approach is its determination that people have no "reasonable expectation of privacy" concerning any information they share with others. When we convey information to another person, the Court has reasoned, we assume the risk that the person will share it with the government. On this theory, people have no expectation of privacy when they dial phone numbers, surf the Web, make a credit card purchase, put out their garbage, or talk with people they think are their friends but are in fact informants. As a result, the Fourth Amendment imposes no restriction on the government obtaining such information and subjecting it to searches for suspicious behavior, even when it has no good reason to suspect a person of wrongdoing.

Before the computer, the government's ability to collect and exploit such information was limited. In the future, the possibilities are likely to be unlimited. Computer searches can be used to identify "suspicious" patterns based on peoples' reading habits, travel, Web surfing, and cell phone records, not to mention their age, sex, race, and religion.

The Court's "third-party disclosure" doctrine is as inapt for the computer age as its property-based approach was for wiretapping. It is simply wrong to equate sharing information with a private corporation as a prerequisite to having a phone or e-mail line, and sharing that information with the government. It is one thing for AOL to know what Web sites you have searched; it is another matter entirely for the federal government to have that information. AOL can't lock you up, and has less reason to harass you for your political views.

As Justice John Marshall Harlan argued in a separate opinion in the *Katz* case, the test of whether the Fourth Amendment is violated should not be merely whether, as a factual matter, society expects a given form of communication to be private, but whether maintaining the privacy of that communication from unwarranted government intrusion is essential to the workings of democracy. On that view, constitutional privacy under the Fourth Amendment is not an objective fact wholly captive to technology, but a social value that we choose to protect despite technological advances.

Jeffrey Rosen suggests that the threats to privacy come not only from technological advances and the courts' failure to confront them, but also from public attitudes. Surveying a wide range of psychological literature, Rosen argues that people are susceptible to powerful irrational fears that compromise their ability to protect their own interests in preserving privacy. Most people, he claims, have "trouble distinguishing improbable events," such as terrorist attacks, "which tend to be the most memorable, from mundane events, which are more likely to repeat themselves." They therefore demand "draconian and symbolic but often poorly designed laws and technologies of surveillance and exposure to eliminate the risks that are, by their nature, difficult to reduce." At the same time, many Americans in the modern age seem to crave exposure more than privacy, as demonstrated, he argues, by the increasing popularity of reality TV, Web logs, and advice books about how to "market" oneself.

The private market only reinforces these tendencies. Rosen shows that the high-tech industry has incentives both to encourage public anxiety about terror threats and to compete for the public dollars that will reward technological "solutions" to the demand for total security. Security is a growth industry; a speaker at a trade electronics forum in Las Vegas estimated that spending on security technologies, including listening devices and databases, will increase by 30 percent a year, reaching $62 billion a year in 2006. Rosen quotes Larry Ellison, Oracle's CEO, who boasts that in the name of advancing national security, his company will create a global database within the next twenty years, "and we're going to track everything."

Rosen agrees with Dash that Fourth Amendment doctrine does not adequately protect privacy in today's high-tech world; but he considers it a waste of time to look to the courts for relief. In his view, history shows that Congress is better situated to protect privacy. While the Supreme Court has radically diluted the protection of privacy and allowed government access to financial and other data through its "third-party disclosure" doctrine, Congress has enacted many statutes protecting privacy despite the Court's decisions, including the Privacy Act, the Fair Credit Reporting Act, the Right to Financial Privacy Act, and the Health Insurance Portability and Accountability Act. These laws restrict government access to financial and health-related data, and impose limits on the government's recording of political communications and other First Amendment activities.

Rosen's confidence in the political process is paradoxical, however, since he also believes that the public today is more interested in publicity than in privacy, and that both the public and the commercial markets favor security over privacy. The only sure thing about Congress is that it will respond to public opinion and market forces.

If there is no possibility of increasing the public's concern about privacy, there is also little hope for Congress.

This brings us back to Dash's plea that the courts intervene on behalf of privacy. Recognizing the risk that the public and the political process may disregard fundamental rights in times of crisis, the Founders protected those values in a constitution that is difficult to change, and made it enforceable by judges with life tenure. The courts have often failed to live up to their responsibility to protect the Bill of Rights but that is no reason not to hold them to it. If Dash may expect too much from the courts, Rosen asks for too little.

The Supreme Court's 2004 decisions rejecting the Bush administration's sweeping assertion of unchecked authority to lock up human beings indefinitely without trial or hearing, illustrate this point. Congress took no steps whatever to confront the president on behalf of the six hundred men held at Guantánamo or the three men held in a brig in South Carolina. Whatever the limitations of its recent decisions, it took the Supreme Court to challenge the president.

The ultimate defender of liberty, however, is neither the Court nor Congress, but the people. In 1931 Judge Learned Hand famously warned Yale Law School graduates that

> Liberty lies in the hearts of men and women; when it dies there, no constitution, no law, no court can save it.... While it lies there it needs no constitution, no law, no court to save it.

Like many memorable quotes, Hand's warning sacrifices nuance for rhetoric. The Constitution, the law, and the courts all serve to remind us of (and therefore to reinforce) our collective commitment to liberty.

But Hand was surely right that we cannot rely *exclusively* on constitutions, courts, or laws. In that light, perhaps the most promising development since September 11 for those who care about principles of liberty and privacy has been the grassroots campaign of the Bill of Rights

Defense Committee. The committee was formed, immediately after the Patriot Act was passed, by civil rights activists in Amherst, Massachusetts, who had what may have seemed the wildly impractical idea of getting local city and town councils to pass resolutions condemning the civil liberties abuses in the act. The committee began its campaign in the places one might expect—Amherst, Northampton, Santa Monica, Berkeley. But today, more than four hundred jurisdictions across the country have adopted such resolutions, including legislatures in eight states— Vermont, Alaska, Maine, California, Idaho, Montana, Colorado, and Hawaii—and many of the nation's biggest cities, including New York, Los Angeles, Chicago, Dallas, Philadelphia, and Washington, D.C.[5]

The resolutions typically condemn not only the surveillance provisions of the Patriot Act—particularly the surveillance of libraries and private records—but also the administration's tactics of mass preventive detention of noncitizens, open-ended imprisonment of "enemy combatants," ethnic profiling, and denials of access to lawyers. Although the resolutions don't have much legal effect, they have huge symbolic and organizing value. Each time a resolution is placed on the agenda of a city council, it provides an opportunity to educate the public about the lengths to which the Bush administration has already gone, about the fundamental values that underlie our constitutional commitments, and about the importance of ordinary people standing up and being heard. While the campaign has not had much attention in the national press and has been largely ignored on television, local politicians and active members of both parties have become well aware of it. And the campaign has helped to create a vast network of citizens concerned about liberty and privacy and ready and willing to speak up in their defense.

---

5. For details on the campaign, see the Bill of Rights Defense Committee's Web site, www.bordc.org, and the ACLU's report, "Independence Day 2003: Main Street America Fights the Federal Government's Insatiable Appetite for New Powers in the Post 9/11 Era," at www.aclu.org.

The quiet success of the Bill of Rights Defense Committee's campaign may well explain the Bush administration's failure to introduce most of what has been dubbed "Patriot II," a draft of which was leaked in February 2003. Among other things, that bill called for presumptively stripping US citizens of their citizenship if they were found to have supported a "terrorist organization." It would also have given the attorney general unreviewable power to deport any nonnationals—presumably including citizens shorn of their citizenship—who, in his opinion, threaten our "national defense, foreign policy, or economic interests."

The campaign of the Bill of Rights Defense Committee may also explain the national tour Ashcroft undertook in 2003 to promote and defend the Patriot Act. When that act was passed six weeks after the September 11 attacks, the vote in the Senate was 98–1.[6] The attorney general did not need to waste his time defending a statute with that kind of support. But it subsequently lost much of that support, thanks in large part to the Bill of Rights Defense Committee. Its campaign also likely had an effect in prompting virtually all of the Democratic presidential candidates in the 2004 election to condemn the Patriot Act. While Congress disappointingly reauthorized the Patriot Act in 2006, the administration faced a much more skeptical Congress at that time, and was forced to accept a number of limits on the act's original grants of authority.

Efforts like those of the Bill of Rights Defense Committee underscore the realities of American politics. If there is any hope for Congress, the courts, or even, in another administration, the executive branch to do something about preserving privacy in the post–September 11 era, ordinary people will have to be mobilized to express their concerns in public. At the same time, the erosion of personal privacy and the erection by the government of walls of secrecy

---

6. Only Wisconsin Senator Russell Feingold voted against it.

make public debate and resistance all the more difficult and risky. Dash and Rosen argue eloquently for the critical need to protect privacy if we are to preserve democracy. They disagree about the institutions most likely to provide those protections. But they agree that it is up to us to hold our government accountable to the values that gave it birth and justify its very existence.

6

ARE WE SAFER?

ACCORDING TO THE JUSTICE DEPARTMENT'S Web site lifeandliberty.gov, we are "winning the war on terrorism with unrelenting focus and unprecedented cooperation." The US government has captured or killed some three thousand al-Qaeda "operatives," including two thirds of its leadership. Among those captured is the alleged mastermind of September 11, Khalid Sheikh Mohammed, from whom the government reportedly obtained substantial intelligence, if only after the use of waterboarding and other forms of torture. The Bush administration says it has disrupted terrorist plots throughout the world—the Web site claims 150, although President Bush in a speech in October 2005 claimed only ten. The government has increased security at the borders and airports. The Justice Department has prosecuted more than four hundred people in "terrorism-related investigations" since September 11, and it has, according to the Web site, obtained convictions or guilty pleas in more than two hundred of these cases. It claims to have broken up terrorist cells in Buffalo, Detroit, Seattle, Portland, Oregon, and northern Virginia. And over 515 foreign nationals linked to the investigation of September 11 have been deported. Most important for Americans, there has not been another terrorist attack on US soil in the more than six years since September 11.

Of course, President Bush also famously proclaimed victory in Iraq, aboard the aircraft carrier USS *Abraham Lincoln* on May 1, 2003. (Shortly thereafter, he announced that "we found the weapons of mass destruction.") Since then, more than four thousand Americans and ten to twenty times as many Iraqis have died in Iraq, and we still haven't found any weapons of mass destruction. So victory proclamations from this administration deserve a strong dose of skepticism.

How does one measure victory in the "global war on terrorism"? In April 2004, the State Department reported that terrorist incidents throughout the world had dropped in the previous year, a fact Deputy Secretary of State Richard L. Armitage promptly cited as "clear evidence that we are prevailing in the fight" against terrorism. Two months later, a chagrined Colin Powell acknowledged that the department had miscounted, and that in fact terrorism worldwide had increased—where the initial report stated that the number of injuries resulting from international terrorist incidents had fallen from 2,013 in 2002 to 1,593 in 2003, the corrected report stated that in fact terrorist-related injuries had risen to 3,646. In 2005, the State Department eliminated numbers from its annual terrorism report, saying they were too difficult to track accurately, but soon thereafter a leak suggested another reason for the omission—government analysts had found that terrorist incidents worldwide had jumped three-fold from 2003 levels, with 651 attacks in 2004 resulting in 1,907 deaths. So much for progress in the global war on terror.

President Bush is fond of repeating, "We are fighting them over there so that we won't have to fight them here at home." As a slogan, this may be good politics. But as a counterterrorism strategy, it appears to be a disaster. Fighting them "over there" has since 2003 meant committing over one hundred thousand troops, hundreds of billions of dollars, and thousands of lives to a conflict in Iraq whose only clear connection to the "war on terror" has been its encouragement of terrorism. The US attack on Iraq has created the world's principal breeding and training ground for anti-American terrorists. Many highly informed commentators have argued that the war in Iraq, based at best on faulty intelligence and at worst on outright lies, was a major diversion from the real enemy—al-Qaeda and the terrorists loosely linked with it, or inspired by it—and that the war with Iraq has therefore made us less secure.[1]

Daniel Benjamin and Steven Simon, counterterrorism experts at the National Security Council under President Clinton, argue in their recent book, *The Next Attack*,[2] that the problem is more deep-rooted than the administration's erroneous venture in Iraq. In their view, the Iraq war is a symptom of the Bush administration's obsession with fighting an offensive "war on terror," an obsession that has caused the administration to disregard the less glamorous but more crucial task of shoring up America's defenses against future attacks. Committed to an outmoded strategy directed at states rather than the loose-knit non-state terrorist movements that actually threaten us, the administration sought out a state to attack, and after an initial and justifiable campaign in Afghanistan, invaded Iraq. But when it comes to fighting the decentralized threat of fundamentalist Islamic terrorism, Benjamin and Simon maintain, the best defense is not a good offense, but a good defense.

Especially after the US and its local allies forced al-Qaeda out of Afghanistan, the threat of fundamentalist Islamic terrorism is not centralized, but globalized and dispersed. The subway bombings in Madrid and London in 2003 and 2005 were the work not of disciplined al-Qaeda agents acting on orders from above but of small bands of young men with little or no connection to al-Qaeda, and

---

1. See, for example, Richard Clarke, *Against All Enemies: Inside America's War on Terror* (Free Press, 2004) and James Fallows, "Bush's Lost Year," *The Atlantic*, October 2004.

2. *The Next Attack: The Failure of the War on Terror and a Strategy for Getting It Right* (Times Books, 2006).

little or no previous record as terrorists. Benjamin and Simon see these attacks as signs of a "new breed of self-starting terrorist cells," and argue that the development of such cells has been vastly facilitated by the Internet. In 1998, they report, there were only twelve Web sites for terrorist groups; in 2005, there were 4,400. The Web sites spread both religious doctrine calling for violence and practical instructions for carrying it out. The consequences have been dire: according to the RAND Corporation, three quarters of all suicide bombings since 1968 took place in the four years after September 11.

Because the terrorist threat is decentralized and globalized, it cannot be fought by traditional military methods. There is no territory to take, no land to occupy, and, with few exceptions, no country to hold accountable. The target is constantly moving and growing. Benjamin and Simon suggest that we think of the terrorist threat as two concentric circles—a relatively small inner one consisting of committed terrorists, violently opposed to what they see as infidel Western governments and institutions, and a larger outer circle consisting of those susceptible of being moved to the inner circle. The challenge, they argue, is not only to find and incapacitate the inner circle, but also to reduce migration from the outer to the inner circle. Or, as Donald Rumsfeld asked in an October 2003 internal Pentagon memo, "Are we capturing, killing or deterring and dissuading more terrorists every day than the madrassas and the radical clerics are recruiting, training and deploying against us?"[3]

Much of Benjamin and Simon's book concentrates on the war with Iraq, which they view as having played into the terrorists' hands. Drawing on their own experience and contacts when they were members of Clinton's National Security Agency, they retell the now-

---

3. Memo from Donald Rumsfeld to Dick Myers et al., "Re: Global War on Terrorism," October 16, 2003, available at www.globalsecurity.org/military/library/policy/dod/rumsfeld-d20031016sdmemo.htm.

familiar story of how the Bush administration was bent on regime change in Iraq almost from the day it took office. It started planning for war against Iraq immediately after the terrorist attacks of September 11; pressured intelligence agencies to make a case for the invasion of Iraq; created its own ad hoc Counter Terrorism Evaluation Group, headed by Douglas Feith, undersecretary of defense for policy, to make the case when the intelligence agencies were reluctant to do so; and then failed to plan for the war's aftermath. According to Benjamin and Simon, administration officials, certain that the US would be welcomed with open arms, literally prohibited planners from even considering the problem of postwar security.

There is little question that the Iraq war, instead of supporting the struggle against terror, has weakened it. In February 2005, CIA Director Porter Goss told Congress that "Islamic extremists are exploiting the Iraqi conflict to recruit new anti-US jihadists," and those "who survive will leave Iraq experienced and focused on acts of urban terrorism. They represent a potential pool of contacts to build transnational terrorist cells, groups, and networks."[4] The military analyst Anthony Cordesman has identified thirty-two "adaptations" to US strategy that the insurgents have successfully made since the war began, including "mixed attacks" in which one bomb follows another with some delay, in order to maximize injury to police and rescue workers; more sophisticated surveillance of US forces and their allies; improved infiltration of the Iraqi military and police forces; and increasingly deadly improvised explosive devices. The insurgents have obtained access to large caches of Saddam Hussein's arms that the US military failed to secure. And they have been able to demonstrate to the world their commitment and their willingness to die by daily attacks on the US and Iraqi military and police forces—many of

---

4. Hearing before the Senate Intelligence Committee, 109th Congress, 1st Session, February 16, 2005.

them suicide attacks that are videotaped and promptly disseminated throughout the world via the Internet.

As Benjamin and Simon put it, the administration "failed the first test of military leadership. They did not know who their real enemy was." The authors cite the constant bombing and heavy ground fire of the "shock and awe" campaign at the beginning of the Iraq war as an illustration of the problem. The bombing was effective for a few weeks in subduing Saddam Hussein. But if the enemy is a terrorist ideology spread throughout the Muslim diaspora, a "shock and awe" strategy is very likely to backfire by reinforcing the enemy's description of the United States as an aggressive force without regard for the lives of innocent Muslims.

National security policy, the authors argue, should reject the model of a military "war on terror," and instead adopt an intelligence-based approach that (1) seeks to identify, capture, and disrupt terrorists; (2) safeguards the most dangerous weapons to keep them out of terrorists' hands; (3) identifies and protects the most vulnerable targets in the US; and (4) reduces the creation of new terrorists by addressing the grievances that drive people to extreme violence in the first place.

The Bush administration's stubborn adherence to the traditional conception of war has caused it to disregard more important and effective defensive actions. The administration, Benjamin and Simon write, has failed to safeguard nuclear weapons materials in the former Soviet Union; failed to identify and protect the most vulnerable targets within the United States, such as water supplies; failed to work effectively with private businesses that are responsible for other vulnerable targets, such as chemical plants; and failed to increase in any significant measure the monitoring of container cargo at shipping ports, of which only one in twenty is inspected. According to the authors, the FBI is still so reluctant to adapt its methods to the realities of terrorism that it has used its intelligence "analysts" to take out the garbage and answer phones, the result being a very large turnover of employees who should be piecing together scraps of intelligence in order to find terrorists and disrupt their plans.

Benjamin and Simon's critique of homeland security is largely corroborated by the bipartisan 9/11 Commission's assessment in December 2005 of the Bush administration's progress in fulfilling the forty-one recommendations in the commission's final report, released in July 2004. Grading the administration on each of its recommended reforms, the 9/11 Commission gave it five F's, twelve D's, eight C's, several incompletes, and only one A–. Among the measures that received either an F or a D are some of the most basic requirements of security. The administration was given a D for its identification of vulnerable potential targets, as well as for its efforts to secure weapons of mass destruction, its screening of checked luggage and cargo for explosives, its arrangements for sharing information among intelligence agencies, and its support of secular educational reform in Muslim countries. It received an F for, among other things, its failure to develop common standards with other nations for detaining and prosecuting terrorist suspects as well as for its failure to establish an effective program to screen airline passengers for potential terrorists.[5]

Benjamin and Simon's diagnosis of the Bush administration as fixated on outdated conceptions of war is ironic, given the administration's insistence that "everything changed" after September 11, and that it has adopted an entirely new model for fighting global terror. For example, the Pentagon's National Security Strategy, issued in September 2002, advanced a new and controversial justification for going to war. It argued that in light of the threats now posed by weapons of mass destruction, war is justified not only when the nation is attacked

---

5. "Final Report on 9/11 Commission Recommendations," December 5, 2005, available at www.9-11pdp.org/press/2005-12-05_report.pdf.

nine were serious offenders—among them, Richard Reid and Zacarias Moussaoui—most were convicted not of terrorist activity but of broad-based charges of association with, or support of, a terrorist group, without any connection to actual terrorist actions.

A Syracuse research institute found that the median sentence handed down in cases labeled "terrorist" by the Justice Department in the first two years after September 11 was only fourteen days, not the kind of sentence that will incapacitate or deter a terrorist.[8] New York University's Center on Law and Security reached a similar conclusion, finding, after reviewing the prosecutions in "terror-related" cases, that "the legal war on terror has yielded few visible results. There have been...almost no convictions on charges reflecting dangerous crimes."[9]

As for the 515 deportations, most were carried out under a policy that barred deportation unless a person was first cleared by the FBI of any connection to terrorism. In identifying actual terrorists, these deportations are misses, not hits.

Virtually all of the cases in which the government has actually charged individuals with a crime relating to terrorism allege not acts of terrorism per se, but only "material support" to a group the government has labeled terrorist, a term expansively defined to include financial assistance, training, services, and even expert advice. Under the statute prohibiting material support, the Bush administration maintains that it need not show that the person it arrests had anything to do with furthering a terrorist act. In one case in which I am representing a human rights group, for example, the government has argued that the law prohibits the group from offering "training"

---

8. See "Criminal Terrorism Enforcement Since the 9/11/01 Attacks," a report issued by the Transactional Records Access Clearinghouse, December 8, 2003, available at trac.syr.edu/tracreports /terrorism/report031208.html.

9. See their report, "Terrorist Trials: A Report Card," February 2005, available at www.law .nyu.edu/centers/lawsecurity /publications/terroristtrialreportcard.pdf.

in human rights advocacy to a Turkish organization, even though the government does not dispute that the intent of the training is precisely to discourage terrorism and encourage peaceful resolution of disputes.

Some of the convictions for "material support" that the administration has obtained seem to have to do more with inflating the numbers shown on its Web site than with any actual threat to national security. A case in point is the prosecution of Lynne Stewart, a sixty-five-year-old criminal defense lawyer in New York City. In June 2000, while representing Sheik Omar Abdel Rahman, who is serving multiple life sentences for conspiring to bomb the bridges and tunnels around Manhattan, Stewart issued a statement from the sheik to the press, and thereby violated an administrative restriction that barred him from contact with the outside world. Before September 11, the government responded, appropriately, by revoking Stewart's visiting privileges and insisting that she sign a more restrictive agreement before visiting the sheik again.

But after September 11, the government charged Stewart with the crime of providing "material support for terrorism." She was convicted in February 2005 after a trial in which the government presented highly prejudicial and largely irrelevant evidence—including a tape from Osama bin Laden, played for the New York jury around the anniversary of the September 11 attacks, even though neither Stewart nor her codefendants were alleged to have had any ties to al-Qaeda. Prosecutors sought a thirty-year sentence, but the judge sentenced Stewart to only twenty-eight months. Her conviction provides another statistic in the Justice Department's effort to show results in the "war on terrorism," but it is difficult to see how it makes Americans safer.

Several of the government's most prominent "terrorist" cases have disintegrated under close scrutiny. John Ashcroft repeatedly claimed that the prosecution of Sami al-Arian, a computer science professor at the University of South Florida, showed why the Patriot Act was essential. Yet after the prosecution presented eighty witnesses and hundreds of hours of taped surveillance over six months of trial, and after al-Arian's lawyers rested their case without calling a single witness, a jury in Tampa found al-Arian not guilty of the most serious charges against him, including conspiracy to murder and to aid a terrorist organization. The jury was deadlocked 10–2 in favor of acquittal on all the rest, including a charge of "material support" and an immigration violation. *Time* magazine quoted a former FBI official who stated that in late 2002 the FBI was pressured to make a case against al-Arian despite weak evidence: "'We were in shock, but those were our marching orders,' [said] the supervisor, who felt that the Justice Department was rushing to indict before it had really appraised the evidence."[10]

The administration earlier claimed to have uncovered an espionage ring at Guantánamo Bay, consisting of a Muslim chaplain and three translators. It charged Captain James Yee, the chaplain, with taking classified information off base—but then dismissed all charges when it could not establish that any of the information was even classified.[11] It brought thirty charges against Ahmed al-Halabi, a twenty-four-year-old translator, some carrying the death penalty, but after ten months dropped all the serious charges and accepted a guilty plea to four minor crimes, including taking pictures at Guantánamo without approval. The plea allowed al-Halabi to go free on the basis of the time served. A third man, Ahmed Fathy Mehalba, also pleaded guilty to minor crimes such as lying to investigators, and was set free a few months later. The government dropped all charges against a fourth man, Jackie Farr.

---

10. Tim Padgett and Wendy Malloy, "When Terror Charges Just Won't Stick," *Time*, December 19, 2005.

11. See Joseph Lelyveld's review of James Yee's book, *For God and Country* (Public Affairs, 2005), in *The New York Review of Books*, December 15, 2005.

The government prosecuted Sami al-Hussayen, a Saudi Arabian student at the University of Idaho, for giving material support to a terrorist group. But when the evidence showed that he had engaged in only speech—he ran a Web site with links to other Web sites, some of which advocated jihad—a jury acquitted him of all terrorism charges. And the administration's first jury conviction for material support to terrorism in a post–September 11 case, in Detroit, was thrown out in September 2004 when the government admitted that the prosecutor had failed to disclose that its principal witness had lied on the stand.

In perhaps its most prominent failure, the administration, when faced with the possibility that it might be held accountable for its actions, abandoned its efforts to hold two US citizens, Jose Padilla and Yaser Hamdi, in military custody as "enemy combatants." After the Supreme Court held that the military had to provide Hamdi a hearing to show why he was detained, the administration simply let him go, on the condition that he return to Saudi Arabia and renounce his citizenship. And when Jose Padilla's lawyers sought Supreme Court review of his detention, the administration suddenly transferred him to civilian criminal custody, where he was convicted not of committing or planning violence, but of playing a marginal part in a nebulous conspiracy to support unnamed terrorist groups.

Despite its aggressively preventive tactics, the administration has yet to identify a single al-Qaeda cell in the US. Its Web site claims to have disrupted terror cells in "Buffalo, Detroit, Seattle, Portland (Oregon), and Northern Virginia," but does not claim that any of these groups were al-Qaeda cells. Those cases include most of the thirty-nine convictions on terror-related charges identified by *The Washington Post*, but they provide no evidence of any internal conspiracy to undertake terrorist attacks on the United States. Several men arrested in northern Virginia were convicted of playing paintball and attending training camps to fight in Kashmir in the conflict between Pakistan and India, not to attack the US. Six men in Portland pleaded guilty to trying to go to Afghanistan to fight alongside the Taliban—they could have been charged with treason, perhaps, but not terrorism.

As for the Buffalo "cell," it consisted of six young men, actually from Lackawanna, a small town near Buffalo, who pleaded guilty to attending an al-Qaeda training camp in Afghanistan long before September 11. But they returned home and, according to the evidence that emerged, engaged in no illegal, much less terrorist, conduct in the US. The claim about Seattle presumably refers to James Ujaama, a black activist held as a material witness and then charged with conspiracy to open a terrorist training camp. He pleaded guilty to making a donation to the Taliban in contravention of an economic embargo imposed before September 11, and was freed after two years in prison. (He was rearrested in 2007 after violating the terms of his plea agreement, and pleaded guilty to the original charges.) And the only "cell" identified in Detroit is the one I have mentioned, in which all charges against three Arab defendants were dismissed.

Meanwhile, the only Islamic fundamentalist convicted for an attempted terrorist act since September 11 is the shoe bomber Richard Reid, captured not through any preventive initiative of the government but because an alert flight attendant noticed a strange-looking man trying to set fire to his shoe. Three people have been convicted of conspiracy to engage in terrorist conduct. Zacarias Moussaoui pleaded guilty in April 2005 to six counts of conspiracy to attack the United States—but of course he was captured not through any post–September 11 "preventive paradigm," but one month before those attacks occurred. Iyman Faris, an Ohio truck driver, allegedly an associate of Khalid Sheikh Mohammed, pleaded guilty to researching how to bring down the Brooklyn Bridge with a single acetylene torch, a plot that raises more questions about Faris's sanity than about US national security. And Ahmed Abu Ali was convicted in November 2005 of conspiring to kill President Bush while Abu Ali was studying abroad in Saudi Arabia. The only person with whom he allegedly discussed the plot was killed by the Saudis, and Abu Ali's conviction rested solely on a confession that he claims was extracted from him by Saudi security services through torture, a practice for which they are well known.

So despite Bush's claims, the "war on terror" at home has resulted in the conviction of few actual terrorists. In Iraq the "war on terror" has in all likelihood resulted in the recruitment and training of more terrorists than have been captured or killed. Benjamin and Simon make it clear that concerns about terrorist attacks throughout the world are often justified; and the convictions in the US suggest that there are at least pockets of ideological resentment here that might pose a threat of violence in the future. But those facts underscore both the necessity for the kind of defensive measures Benjamin and Simon and the 9/11 Commission have shown are lacking, and the importance of avoiding initiatives that might move people from the outer circle of fundamentalism to the inner circle of terrorists that Benjamin and Simon describe.

It is possible, of course, that some of the administration's measures have produced valuable intelligence, although if that were the case one would expect to see more successful prosecutions for terrorism. It's also possible that these initiatives have deterred some terrorists here from planning attacks on targets in the US and others from coming to the US to do so—but the government has so far produced no evidence that this has been the case.

What can be known is that the administration's tactics—a curious amalgam of outmoded thinking and dangerous new ideas—have created unprecedented levels of distrust toward US law enforcement within the Arab and Muslim communities here as well as intense anti-Americanism abroad. The administration is accurately perceived as unfairly targeting innocent Arabs and Muslims, using coercion against them preemptively and without a solid case, and disregarding fundamental principles of the rule of law and human rights. In the long run the resentment provoked by these measures is the greatest threat to our national security, and the most likely source of the next attack.

7

HOW TO SKIP THE CONSTITUTION

LIKE EVERYTHING ELSE, the Constitution has changed since September 11. So Richard Posner argues in his latest book, *Not a Suicide Pact: The Constitution in a Time of National Emergency*.[1] Posner, a distinguished judge on the US Court of Appeals for the Seventh Circuit and the most prolific legal scholar of his generation, insists that the Constitution has changed sufficiently since September 11 to sanction virtually all of the Bush administration's counterterrorism measures, including coercive interrogation, incommunicado detention, warrantless wiretapping, and ethnic profiling.

The only action by the Bush administration that Posner finds unconstitutional is its short-lived attempt to deny judicial review to US citizens in military custody in the US on grounds that they are "enemy combatants"—a position the administration itself abandoned after the US Court of Appeals for the Fourth Circuit, the most conservative court in the country, dismissed the argument as a "dangerous" proposition. Indeed, Posner's Constitution would permit the administration to go even further than it has—among other things, he defends indefinite preventive detention, the banning of Islamic jihadist rhetoric, mass wiretapping of the entire nation, and making it

---

1. Oxford University Press, 2006.

a crime for newspapers to publish classified information, as when *The Washington Post* broke the story of the CIA's "black sites" or when *The New York Times* disclosed the existence of the National Security Agency's warrantless wiretapping program. All of these are permissible, Posner argues, because unless the Constitution "bends" in the face of threats to our national security, it "will break." When Posner is finished bending the Constitution to reach these results, however, one might justifiably ask what is left to preserve from breaking.

Other federal judges, deciding actual cases or controversies, have found plenty that they concluded was unconstitutional about the administration's antiterror campaign since September 11. Courts have declared unconstitutional statutes making it a crime to provide "expert advice," "services," and "training" to groups designated by the government as terrorist. A provision of the Patriot Act authorizing the FBI to demand information by sending "national security letters," a form of administrative subpoena issued without court review, was ruled unconstitutional because it barred recipients from informing anyone—including a lawyer or a court—of the fact that they had been subpoenaed. Several courts held unconstitutional Attorney General John Ashcroft's directive to try hundreds of immigrants in secret proceedings closed to the public, the press, legal observers, and even their families.

Other judges held unconstitutional a regulation issued shortly after September 11 permitting immigration prosecutors to keep immigrants locked up even after immigration judges had found no basis for their detention and had ordered their release. Most significantly, the Supreme Court ruled unconstitutional the administration's refusal to allow Yaser Hamdi, a US citizen captured in Afghanistan, a hearing in which he could challenge the official determination that he was an "enemy combatant." And in August 2006, a court declared unconstitutional President Bush's secret order authorizing the NSA to conduct warrantless wiretapping within the United States.

Judge Posner is not troubled by any of these measures, at least as a constitutional matter. His theory of the Constitution is at once candid and cavalier. Rejecting popular conservative attacks on "judicial activism," he argues that in view of the open-ended character of many of the document's most important terms—"reasonable" searches and seizures, "due process of law," "equal protection," and even "liberty" itself —it is not objectionable but inevitable that constitutional law is made by judges. He dismisses the constitutional theories of textualism and originalism favored by many conservative judges and scholars as canards, arguing that neither the Constitution's text nor the history of its framing gives much guidance in dealing with most of the hard questions of the day. Constitutional law, he maintains, "is intended to be a loose garment; if it binds too tightly, it will not be adaptable to changing circumstances."

But Posner then goes on to treat the Constitution as essentially a license to open-ended "balancing" of interests by the political branches and the courts. His thinking is informed largely by an economist's predilection for cost-benefit analysis and a philosophical enthusiasm for pragmatism. Posner's reputation as a scholar rests not on his contributions to constitutional theory, but on his role as one of the founding fathers of the movement that applied economic analysis to law. His new book might just as well have been called "An Economist Looks at the Constitution." In the end, constitutional interpretation for Posner is little more than a balancing act, and when the costs of a catastrophic terrorist attack are placed on the scale, he almost always feels they outweigh concerns about individual rights and liberties.

Consider, for example, his views on electronic surveillance. The Bush administration currently faces several dozen lawsuits challenging various aspects of its NSA spying program, which, according to the administration, involves the warrantless wiretapping of international phone calls and e-mails where one of the participants is thought to be connected with al-Qaeda or affiliated groups. That program, as I and many other constitutional scholars have argued, violates a provision in the Foreign Intelligence Surveillance Act (FISA) specifying that it is a crime for officials not to seek a warrant from the appropriate court before engaging in such wiretapping.[2] The Bush administration seeks to justify this violation of law by invoking an inherent presidential power to ignore congressional legislation, echoing President Richard Nixon's defense of his own decision to authorize warrantless wiretapping during the Vietnam War: "When the president does it, that means that it is not illegal." Posner not only sees nothing wrong with the NSA program; he would also find constitutional a far more sweeping measure that subjected every phone call and e-mail in the nation, domestic as well as international, to initial computer screening for patterns of suspicious words, and then permitted intelligence agents to follow up on all communications that the computer treated as suspicious.

How does Posner reach the conclusion that the Constitution would permit such an Orwellian scheme, far more invasive than the Bush administration, if it is to be believed, has been willing to undertake so far? In a word, balancing. In Posner's view, the costs to personal liberty of such a program are minimal, and are outweighed by the benefits to our security. Having a computer analyze one's phone calls is no big deal, he claims, as long as we know it's only looking for terrorists. He admits that there might be a danger of misuse of the information by the agents who follow up on the computer's "suspects," but he considers that risk minimal because he is confident that any such abuse would likely come to light and be widely criticized. (He fails to acknowledge that whistleblowing would be far less likely if he had his way and an Official Secrets Act were passed making it a crime to publish leaked government secrets.) As for the benefits of such surveillance, Posner surmises that such a program might sweep up sufficient

---

2. See the Appendix, "On NSA Spying: A Letter to Congress."

data to permit intelligence agents to "connect the dots" and prevent a catastrophic attack. Even if it didn't, he writes, it would at least have the salutary effect of discouraging terrorists from communicating by telephone and e-mail.

Every aspect of Posner's analysis is open to question. He ignores that privacy is essential to political freedom: if everyone knows that their every electronic communication is subject to government monitoring, even by a computer, it would likely have a substantial chilling effect on communications that the government might conceivably find objectionable, not just terrorist planning, and not just criminal conduct. Moreover, Posner ignores the myriad ways in which the government can harass people without its ill intent ever coming to light. For example, the government can selectively prosecute minor infractions of the law, launch arbitrary tax investigations, and engage in blackmail, all methods perfected by FBI Director J. Edgar Hoover. Contrary to Posner's claims, one cannot, as the FBI's abuses showed, trust public scrutiny to forestall such tactics, even in the absence of an Official Secrets Act. Finally, it is far from clear that such a program would be effective—the sheer volume of "dots" generated would make connecting them virtually impossible. In any case, computer programs would be relatively easy to evade through the use of code words.

The real answer to Posner's notion of balance, however, is not to show that a different balance can be struck, but to return to established Fourth Amendment jurisprudence, which has long required that searches must generally be justified by a showing of objective, specific suspicion approved by a judge who is willing to issue a specific warrant. The requirements that a warrant be issued and that it be based on "probable cause" are designed to protect privacy unless there are fairly strong grounds for official intrusion. The principal evil that the Fourth Amendment was drafted to avoid was the "general warrant," which permitted government officials to search anyone's home, without suspicion of specific individuals. Posner's program is nothing less than a twenty-first-century version of exactly what the Fourth Amendment was designed to forbid. Through an open-ended and inevitably subjective balancing of privacy and security, he has managed to turn the Fourth Amendment on its head.

Posner's analysis of coercive interrogation is similarly flawed. Here he incorrectly asserts that the prohibition on coerced confessions is predicated on the Fifth Amendment privilege against compelled self-incrimination; this privilege, he believes, would not apply if coerced testimony is used only for intelligence purposes, and not to incriminate the person interrogated. Here Posner disregards a long line of Supreme Court decisions banning "involuntary" confessions not on grounds of self-incrimination but because the methods of interrogation themselves were found to violate due process of law. Applying this due process test, the Court has consistently ruled that any tactics that compelled a suspect to speak against his will violated due process, even where other evidence showed that the coerced confession was reliable.[3]

Ignoring these cases, Posner discusses only *Rochin v. California*, which held that the Fifth Amendment's due process clause was violated when police pumped a suspect's stomach in the hospital to search for drugs that he had allegedly swallowed. The Court found that such tactics "shock the conscience," because they are "too close to the rack and screw." As Posner concedes, if stomach-pumping in a hospital is too close to the rack and screw, most coercive interrogation tactics would seem to be impermissible as well. But he seeks to distinguish the *Rochin* decision from coercive questioning of suspected terrorists primarily on the ground that it involved the investigation of drug smuggling, which he considers a relatively minor crime. He maintains that greater coercion may be permissible where terrorism is

---

3. See, for example, *Rogers* v. *Richmond*, 365 U.S. 534 (1961); *Watts* v. *Indiana*, 338 U.S. 49 (1949); *Ashcroft* v. *Tennessee*, 327 U.S. 274 (1946).

the subject of investigation. According to his idea of balance, the greater the value of the information sought, the more coercion we should find acceptable without shocking our conscience. But of course one generally does not know the real value of the information before the coercion is applied; and Posner is talking about interrogations for intelligence-gathering purposes, which are by their nature much more open-ended than investigations of suspected criminals.

There is some limit to Posner's attempts at balancing. He would draw the line at torture, at least as a formal legal matter. But he does not explain why he's willing to draw a bright line there while balancing away all coercion short of torture if the information sought is sufficiently valuable. Moreover, he quickly takes away with one hand what he has given with the other, arguing that "in the present context, [there] is a compelling argument for defining torture extremely narrowly, so that necessary violations of the law against torture do not become routine." That's exactly what John Yoo did for Alberto Gonzales in the now infamous August 2002 Office of Legal Counsel "torture memo," in which Yoo defined the criminal ban on torture extremely narrowly, in order to free the CIA to use harsh interrogation tactics on terror suspects. Yoo claimed that the ban on torture did not, for example, forbid interrogators to threaten suspects with death, as long as the death threatened was not imminent. Nor did the ban on torture bar US officials from inflicting extreme physical pain, as long as it fell short of the level associated with organ failure or death.

In an earlier book, *Catastrophe: Risk and Response*, which similarly advocated extensive sacrifices of civil liberties in the hope of averting catastrophic attacks, Posner himself convincingly explained why a balancing approach to coercive interrogation is dangerous. There, as here, he drew the line at torture, but failed to offer any rationale for distinguishing torture from lesser forms of coercive interrogation. In *Catastrophe*, Posner argued against creating an exception to the rule against torture, even where necessary to defuse a "ticking time bomb," on the ground that officials would soon press the outer limits of the permission, "and the practice of torture, once it was thus regularized by judicial demarcation of those bounds, would be likely to become regular within them, ceasing to be an exceptional practice and setting the stage for further extensions." It is, he writes, a short ride down the slippery slope:

> One begins with the extreme case—the terrorist with plague germs or an A-bomb the size of an orange in his Dopp kit, or the kidnapper who alone can save his victim's life by revealing the victim's location. So far, so good; but then the following reflections are invited: if torture is legally justifiable when the lives of thousands are threatened, what about when the lives of hundreds are threatened, or tens? And the kidnap victim is only one. By such a chain of reflections one might be persuaded to endorse a rule that torture is justified if, all things considered, the benefits, which will often be tangible (lives, or a life, saved), exceed the costs, which will often be nebulous.[4]

What is true of torture is equally true of physical coercion short of torture. Posner's advocacy of a balancing approach, allowing officials to calibrate their coercion to the expected value of the information sought, would create the very risks he warned of in his earlier book.

Here, too, the Constitution does not trust government officials to balance in some ad hoc fashion the value of the information they hope to obtain from suspects against the harms their tactics may inflict—on the suspect, on themselves, and on society at large. Instead, due process has long been understood to identify certain fundamental rights that are integral to civilized society. One of those is the prohibition on torture and cruel, inhuman, and degrading

---

4. *Catastrophe: Risk and Response* (Oxford University Press, 2004), pp. 240–241.

treatment—a principle reflected in the Geneva Conventions, an international treaty that virtually every nation in the world has ratified, and the Supreme Court's own rulings on due process, which have for decades prohibited coercive interrogation in criminal investigations.

More generally, the problem with Posner's approach is that it does away with the animating idea of the Constitution—namely, that it represents a collective commitment to principles. The genius behind the Constitution is precisely the recognition that "pragmatic" cost-benefit decisions will often appear in the short term to favor actions that may turn out in the long term to be contrary to our own best principles. Just as we may be tempted to smoke a cigarette tonight despite the fact that in the long term we are likely to suffer as a result, so we know collectively that in the short term we are likely to empower government to suppress unpopular speech, invade the privacy of "dangerous" minorities, and abuse suspected criminals, even though in the long term such actions undermine the values of free speech, equality, and privacy that are necessary to a humane democratic society. If we were always capable of rationally assessing the costs and benefits in such a way as to maximize our collective well-being, short-term and long-term, we might not need a Constitution. But knowing that societies, like individuals, will be tempted to act in ways that undermine their own best interests, we have committed ourselves to a set of constitutional constraints on open ended pragmatic balancing. Posner's view that the Constitution must be bent to the point of sanctioning coercive interrogation and mass warrantless wiretapping reduces the Constitution to a commitment to balance costs and benefits as he (and Attorney General Gonzales) sees them. If that were all there was to it, we would not need a Bill of Rights.

Constitutional theory, in other words, demands more than mere ad hoc balancing. While differing interests and inevitable trade-offs among those interests mean that at some level a balance must be struck between competing claims, constitutional analysis is not an invitation to the freewheeling calculations of the economist. Instead, it requires an effort, guided by text, precedent, and history, to identify the higher principles that guide us as a society, principles so important that they take precedence over the decisions of democratically elected officials. The judge's constitutional duty was perhaps best captured by Justice John Marshall Harlan, writing about the due process clause:

> Due process has not been reduced to any formula; its content cannot be determined by reference to any code. The best that can be said is that through the course of this Court's decisions it has represented the balance which our Nation, built upon postulates of respect for the liberty of the individual, has struck between that liberty and the demands of organized society. If the supplying of content to this Constitutional concept has of necessity been a rational process, it certainly has not been one where judges have felt free to roam where unguided speculation might take them. The balance of which I speak is the balance struck by this country, having regard to what history teaches are the traditions from which it developed as well as the traditions from which it broke. That tradition is a living thing. A decision of this Court which radically departs from it could not long survive, while a decision which builds on what has survived is likely to be sound. No formula could serve as a substitute, in this area, for judgment and restraint.[5]

In Harlan's view, the balance to be struck is not simply the economist's best estimate of the costs and benefits associated with a particular government practice—that, after all, is what politicians do—but the judge's attempt, informed by text, tradition, precedent, and reason, to identify and enforce those principles that rise above day-to-

---

5. *Poe* v. *Ullman*, 367 U.S. 497, 542 (1961; Justice Harlan dissenting).

day cost benefit analysis. Posner's method would discard the constitutional tradition evoked by Harlan and substitute a balancing approach that he admits ultimately involves the weighing of imponderables, and looks remarkably like the "unguided speculation" Harlan correctly rejected.

Posner's rejoinder is that because terrorism in the twenty-first century poses the risk of truly catastrophic harm, it renders constitutional precedent and history largely irrelevant. Everything has changed. We are in a new situation, in which, as Alberto Gonzales said of the Geneva Conventions, the old rules now appear "quaint" or "obsolete." But each new generation faces unforeseen issues. The advent of modern weapons in the early twentieth century changed war as we know it; so did development of the nuclear bomb. International communism backed by the Soviet Union posed a "new" threat of totalitarian takeover. This is not to deny that there is now a real threat that terrorists may get their hands on weapons of mass destruction. But it is to insist that we should be skeptical of claims that because the threat is in some sense "new," history is irrelevant. The principles developed and applied over two centuries to questions of liberty and security should still be central in guiding us as we address the threats of modern terrorists.

The corollary to Posner's pragmatic and utilitarian balancing approach to the Constitution is that judges should defer to the elected legislators and to government officials acting under orders of the president. Judges have no special expertise in national security, he argues, while the political branches of government do. Decisions invalidating security measures as unconstitutional reduce our flexibility, since they are extremely difficult to change through the political process, and may prevent the government from undertaking some kinds of investigation and interrogation. But the Constitution was explicitly meant to reduce our flexibility by cutting off certain questionable actions by government. Trying terrorist criminals without a jury, locking them up without access to a judge, convicting them without proving guilt beyond a reasonable doubt, searching them without probable cause or a warrant, and subjecting them to torture: all these measures might make the terrorists' task more difficult.[6] But because of our Constitution, they are off limits. The Constitution may not be a "suicide pact," but nor is it a license to do anything our leaders think on balance might improve our safety.

In defense of judicial deference to the political branches, Posner reassures his readers, "the Republican Congress has not been a rubber stamp for the national security initiatives of the Bush administration." The record suggests otherwise, and it is troubling that Posner ignores it. Congress has largely stood by passively in the face of sweeping assertions of executive power, and when it has intervened, it has either been to give the executive branch more power or to enact toothless symbolic measures that pose no obstacle to the administration. Thus Congress took no action even when President Bush claimed the power to lock up US citizens indefinitely without charges or trial as "enemy combatants"; it took the Supreme Court, in *Hamdi* v. *Rumsfeld*, to step in and demand due process. Shortly after September 11, Congress passed the Patriot Act, giving the executive broad new powers and reducing judicial oversight, and imposed only a few minor modifications on the administration's initial proposal. Such actions might seem excusable in the intense heat of the moment—but four years later, with plenty of time for deliberation, Congress calmly reenacted the Patriot Act virtually unchanged, just as many of its surveillance provisions were about to expire. In the summer of 2006, when Congress passed the McCain Amendment with majorities too large to veto, it seemed to block the president from imposing cruel,

---

6. As I have argued in these pages, however, many of these shortcuts actually help the terrorists and make us more vulnerable, primarily because of the backlash they create. See Chapter Six, "Are We Safer?"

inhuman, and degrading treatment on foreign nationals held abroad. But that law included no mechanism for enforcement of violations, and it simultaneously denied prisoners the ability to seek habeas corpus review to challenge such treatment.

The historical record is no better. Congress, after all, passed the Alien and Sedition Acts, the World War I statutes that made it a crime to speak out against the war, as well as the anti-Communist laws that laid the groundwork for the McCarthy era. Congress took no action to prevent President Roosevelt's internment of Japanese-Americans during World War II. In fact, one is hard-pressed to identify a single instance in which Congress has imposed a significant constraint on the president during a national security crisis.

Most recently, the Republican Congress again proved itself precisely the rubber stamp that Posner says it is not, when it enacted the Military Commissions Act (MCA). The law was a response to the Supreme Court's landmark decision in *Hamdan* v. *Rumsfeld*, which declared that the tribunals that President Bush created to try alleged war criminals at Guantánamo violated both congressional statutes and the Geneva Conventions. Some Republican senators—especially John McCain and Lindsay Graham—made a big show of standing up to the administration. But they ultimately capitulated, giving the administration almost everything it wanted. In the end, it seemed that the senators' stand was largely for show.

The MCA permits the president to try foreign nationals as enemy combatants before military tribunals that will consider coerced testimony, hearsay, and summaries of classified information that the defendant will have no effective opportunity to confront—just as the rules previously struck down by the Supreme Court had permitted. Instead of requiring the president to make US tribunals conform to the Geneva Conventions, Congress simply declared that in its view the procedures fully satisfy the Geneva Conventions. If courts would disagree, we may never know it. Congress insulated its declaration from judicial review by barring anyone from invoking the Geneva Conventions in court against a federal official or the United States government.

The MCA also weakens the prohibitions on coercive interrogation of prisoners of war. Before enactment of the MCA, the federal War Crimes Act made any violation of Common Article 3 of the Geneva Conventions a criminal offense, including any "cruel treatment" of a detainee. Congress has now amended the War Crimes Act to limit its reach to specified "grave breaches" of the law, notably *not* including all "cruel treatment" of prisoners. Instead, the MCA limits criminal sanctions to those who torture prisoners of war or inflict suffering virtually identical to that associated with torture. As if reflecting the views of John Yoo and Richard Posner, Congress narrowly defined "war crimes" in order to free the CIA to resume its practice of "disappearing" suspected terrorists into undisclosed "black sites" and subjecting them to harsh interrogation tactics, including long periods of being forced to stand naked in frigid rooms while being doused regularly with ice-cold water.

Finally, the MCA seeks to prevent courts from exercising any authority over most aspects of US treatment of war prisoners. In addition to barring prisoners from invoking the Geneva Conventions in court, the law eliminates habeas corpus jurisdiction for those held as "unlawful enemy combatants," a term defined in wholly circular language as anyone found to be an unlawful enemy combatant by a "competent tribunal" established by the president. The cases of such persons are relegated to limited judicial review in the US Court of Appeals for the D.C. Circuit—review that cannot consider claims that the prisoners are being tortured or otherwise abused, and that may not be able to engage in any factual inquiry into whether the prisoners were in fact fighting for the enemy.

Whether the Supreme Court will accept that it has no right to question Congress's rubber stamp of executive power remains to be seen. If it were up to Richard Posner, we could be sure of the result. The Constitution for him is a flexible document; al-Qaeda poses a grave threat; and the courts should defer to the political branches on the balance to be struck. But the Constitution embodies a commitment to principle over ad hoc judgments alleged to be pragmatic, and in particular to the principles of liberty, equality, and dignity, which cannot easily be balanced away. It is precisely because the political branches are so quick to forget this central consideration, especially when fear is high and the rights (and here, lives) of nonconstituents are on the line, that we must insist on a Constitution of principle, enforced by judges who will not take the easy road of deference to other branches or the subjective method of open-ended balancing. Whether judges today are willing to stand up for principle against power has become one of the most urgent questions facing our nation.

8

IN CASE OF EMERGENCY

IT HAS BEEN MORE THAN SIX YEARS since September 11, 2001, and thus far the United States has been spared another terrorist attack on home soil. That's just about the point when cancer patients in remission are told they can begin to relax if their symptoms have not recurred. But with the threat of terrorist attacks, we may never be able to let down our guard. Even if we were to eliminate al-Qaeda altogether—and some counterterrorism experts suggest that we may never know when that day has come, because al-Qaeda is more a loose-knit ideological movement than a distinct and coherent organization—there are always likely to be groups that resent the United States, and are willing to use violence to express their resentment. The issue is not so much Islamic fundamentalism as technological progress. The development of weapons of mass destruction—a development we pioneered—has made it increasingly easier for small groups or even people acting alone to inflict devastating damage. As Yale Law School professor Bruce Ackerman observes in *Before the Next Attack*,[1] the state has lost its monopoly on the deployment of destructive technologies.

In this respect, the threat of terrorist attacks may be something

---

1. *Before the Next Attack: Preserving Civil Liberties in an Age of Terrorism* (Yale University Press, 2006).

that we must learn to live with—as a cancer patient learns to live with the ever-present possibility of recurrence. This feature of terrorism, however, only makes it all the more important that we adopt means for addressing it that are consistent with our deepest principles. The threat of terrorist attack is not a short-term phenomenon requiring temporary sacrifices, with the promise of an eventual return to normalcy, but a long-term condition. It is, as Vice President Dick Cheney has put it, "the new normal."

The fact that the terrorist threat is unlikely to abate anytime soon —or ever—makes a "war on terror" like no other war. While it is never possible, in the midst of a war, to say when it will end, this war may literally have no end. President Bush has said that the war "will not end until every terrorist group of global reach has been found, stopped, and defeated." That day will never arrive.

Many critics have argued that for these reasons, we must resist the label of the "war on terror." Once such rhetoric takes hold, those who care about civil liberties and civil rights will forever be on the defensive. The question is, what is the alternative?

Bruce Ackerman, one of the most creative legal minds of our generation, echoes the critics' concern about war talk and, to his credit, proposes an alternative—the "Emergency Constitution." Al-Qaeda's terrorist attacks, he argues, should be viewed neither as acts of war, as the administration has treated them, nor as mere crimes, as some civil liberties advocates have argued, but as something in between—armed attacks causing a political "emergency." Such attacks, he claims, do not pose an "existential threat" to the nation; there is no risk that al-Qaeda will assume governmental power. They do, however, challenge the nation's "effective sovereignty," by calling into question the government's ability to protect its people.

As a result, he suggests, neither a war model nor a business-as-usual model is apt. Rather, we need to authorize temporary emergency authorities in order to reassure a panicked citizenry that the state will swiftly restore order and maintain control. Otherwise, he warns, the government will inevitably overreact, employing rhetoric about war to justify extraordinary measures that undermine civil liberties. And with each attack, the overreaction will go further. Ackerman boldly claims that all of the world's constitutions, including our own, are defective in failing adequately to address such political emergencies, and proposes nothing less than a change in constitutional system.

Ackerman's skepticism of war rhetoric is well founded. His proposals, moreover, have been taken seriously. Among the legal authorities who have praised his book are Philip Heymann, a former US deputy attorney general, now a professor of law at Harvard, and Eugene Fidell, the president of the National Institute of Military Justice, who credits him with having written "a politically astute—and courageous—plan for preserving our constitutional system." Unfortunately, while Ackerman's diagnosis of the problem is incisive, his proposal would do nothing to cure it. When stripped of its own rhetoric, what Ackerman presents as a solution to an asserted constitutional defect turns out to be little more than a flawed preventive detention law. Far from solving the problem of overzealous responses to terrorist threats, Ackerman's proposal would likely exacerbate the problem, by freeing government officials to round up thousands of "terror suspects" without having to satisfy any court that there is any factual basis for the detentions. And his plan would do nothing to stop government officials from asserting extraordinary powers and undermining basic freedoms using other legal authorities.

Instead of the prompt judicial review that the Constitution generally requires when suspects are locked up, Ackerman would subject emergency preventive detention to an unusual legislative restraint. Borrowing from South Africa's constitution, which requires a 60 percent majority to sustain emergency powers, Ackerman would require the legislature to renew the emergency—and therefore the emergency authority to detain—at two-month intervals by increasingly lopsided "supermajorities." Initially, the legislature need only ratify the emergency by a simple majority, but after two months, continuation of the emergency would require a 60 percent majority; after four months a 70 percent majority would be necessary; and after six months 80 percent of the legislature would have to approve. This "supermajoritarian escalator," as Ackerman calls it, would institutionalize a presumption against prolonged emergencies, for without an overwhelming consensus, emergencies would be short-lived.

As long as the state of emergency is in effect, the president would have the power to lock up suspects for forty-five days, or until the emergency is terminated, whichever comes sooner. Upon an individual's arrest the government would have to make a "showing" in court of facts to justify its actions, but the court would have no power to assess the sufficiency of that showing. At no time during his period of incarceration would the suspect have any opportunity to challenge the evidentiary grounds for his detention. He would be able to seek judicial intervention only to bar the use of torture. At the end of the forty-five-day period, the government would have to release the suspect or charge him criminally. Those who are not charged or who are acquitted in a subsequent criminal trial would be compensated at a rate of $500 a day (or $22,500 for a prison term of forty-five days). Punitive damages would also be available, but only if prosecutors could be shown to have lied in seeking to justify a detention.

The idea behind the proposal is to give the president short-term emergency powers that will reassure the public and help forestall a second terrorist attack, while sharply limiting the period of the emergency in order to preserve civil liberties for the long term.

But Ackerman's proposal is fundamentally flawed for three reasons. First, there is no reason to believe that preventive detention without judicial review is either necessary or sufficient to protect us from a second attack. Whatever limited protection preventive detention might promise could be achieved without the drastic step of eliminating judicial review. Second, the existence of such a provision would not forestall other abuses of civil liberties in the name of national security. Third, the proposal rests on a preference for legislative checks over judicial checks on questions of emergency powers and individual liberties, and that preference is unsupported by the factual record we have. While far from perfect, the courts have been more reliable than Congress when it comes to protecting the rights of the most vulnerable. Ackerman is right that we need credible alternatives to war talk, but his own alternative fails the test of plausibility.

The historical record should caution us against encouraging widespread preventive detention in the name of national security. On three occasions, US authorities have resorted to mass preventive detention in periods of crisis. After eight bombs exploded in eight American cities within the same hour in 1919, the Justice Department launched what became known as the "Palmer Raids," even though they were planned by the young J. Edgar Hoover. Government officials rounded up thousands of foreign nationals on charges of technical immigration violations or association with Communist organizations, interrogated them without lawyers, and deported hundreds. None was found to have had any involvement in the bombings.

In World War II, President Franklin Delano Roosevelt authorized the internment of 110,000 persons of Japanese descent, more than 70,000 of whom were American citizens. The stated purpose was to forestall espionage or sabotage by Japanese and Japanese-Americans living on the West Coast. Not one of the internees was found to have been a spy or to have planned any sabotage.

After the attacks of September 11, Attorney General John Ashcroft launched the nation's third mass preventive detention campaign. In seven weeks, the government arrested over a thousand so-called "terror suspects." During the first two years after September 11, the government imprisoned more than five thousand foreign nationals in preventive detention as part of its "war on terror." Virtually all were Arab and Muslim. Many were arrested and tried in secret. Most were arrested on technical immigration charges, and many were held long after their immigration cases were fully resolved. Nearly five years later, not one of the five thousand stands convicted of a terrorist offense.

Ackerman responds that the mere fact that preventive detention did not work in the past does not mean that it won't work in the future. It is "*perfectly* possible" that a dragnet might actually net a potential terrorist, he writes. But that is a terribly thin hope upon which to rest such an awesome power. Moreover, what all of the previous roundups had in common was that they did not require proof that the individuals detained posed any threat. Ackerman's proposal would do the same thing.

When Ackerman first proposed his idea in a *Yale Law Journal* article entitled "The Emergency Constitution," he called for preventive detention without any requirement that the government demonstrate any basis for suspicion. I wrote a reply, in which I criticized that aspect of his proposal.[2] In response, Ackerman has now modified his proposal to provide that detention should be based on "reasonable suspicion" that a person may be engaged in an illegal act. That standard comes from a Supreme Court case permitting police to stop people briefly in public places in order to dispel or confirm their "reasonable suspicion" that a crime may be afoot.[3] The Court concluded that because such brief stops are an important method for investigating potential crime, and impose only a minimal temporary intrusion, they may be carried out when the police have "reasonable suspicion" rather than "probable cause" of a crime. What is "reasonable suspicion"? The

---

2. See Bruce Ackerman, "The Emergency Constitution," *Yale Law Journal*, Vol. 113 (2004), p. 1029; David Cole, "The Priority of Morality: The Emergency Constitution's Blind Spot," *Yale Law Journal*, Vol. 113 (2004), p. 1753.

3. *Terry v. Ohio*, 392 U.S. (1968).

Court has said that it's "more than a hunch"; but it has also held that if a person runs away from the police in a high-crime area, that behavior is sufficient to meet the standard of "reasonable suspicion."

Whether a standard of suspicion created to justify temporary stops on public streets should be sufficient to warrant forty-five days of incarceration, as Ackerman proposes, raises a serious constitutional question. But the more fundamental problem is that even this minimal standard is meaningless if judges cannot enforce it. Under Ackerman's proposal, a person wrongfully arrested on less than "reasonable suspicion" would have no recourse to a court while he was being held in jail. Nor would the presence or absence of "reasonable suspicion" affect compensation afterward. Upon release, those wrongfully arrested without "reasonable suspicion" would be entitled to no greater compensation than those lawfully arrested with "reasonable suspicion."

Compensation in Ackerman's scheme turns not on whether there was any basis for the detention in the first place, but only on whether a person is successfully prosecuted for a crime thereafter. Thus, those arrested without any legitimate basis get no compensation so long as prosecutors can convict them of even the most minor offense—from credit card fraud to a false statement on a government form. And those who are acquitted or never charged will get full compensation even if there was a legitimate basis for suspecting them at the time of detention. Accordingly, Ackerman's addition of a "reasonable suspicion" standard does not work, because literally nothing turns on whether the government complies with it.

This is not to suggest that preventive detention should be flatly prohibited. Most liberal democracies have preventive detention laws, and the United States already permits preventive detention of those awaiting trial or deportation hearings who pose a danger to others or a risk of flight, as well as those who are dangerous to others or mentally ill. A carefully formulated preventive detention law, preserving prompt judicial review, and restricting resort to other laws that have been abused for preventive detention purposes in the past, might lead to fewer innocents wrongly detained while preserving the authority to hold the truly dangerous. But there is no reason to believe that a preventive detention law that, in effect, authorizes arrest without grounds for suspicion would make us any safer. And it would give official approval to the mass detention of innocents.

Ackerman's proposal also fails to meet his goal of preventing more radical abuses of civil liberties. In his view, the preventive detention provision will somehow satisfy the government and the public that an emergency will be adequately addressed, and will therefore reduce the risk that Congress or the president will seek still broader powers. This is no more than wishful thinking, and again, it is directly contrary to the historical evidence. Ackerman portrays his "state of emergency" as something "new," but there is in fact nothing new about emergency power. As Ackerman acknowledges, the Romans gave the executive special powers during states of emergency, and most European constitutions do so to this day. US law has long provided for emergency powers. In the twentieth century alone, Congress passed some 470 laws delegating emergency powers to the president, yet their existence did not protect us from abuses of civil liberties.

American law currently includes a wide range of emergency powers. Indeed, citing the National Emergencies Act, President Bush declared an emergency just twelve days after the attacks of September 11. On the basis of that declaration, he has used emergency powers to freeze the assets of anyone he labels a "specially designated terrorist," without charges of wrongdoing, hearings, or trials, and he has authorized other government officials to add to this blacklist anyone "otherwise associated" with those on the list—again regardless of wrongdoing and without notice, hearing, or trial. Yet the availability of such extraordinary emergency powers did nothing to stop the administration from invoking a "war on terror" and adopting a raft of other measures that radically infringe on civil liberties—from wire-tapping without a warrant to indefinite incommunicado detention to torture.

Part of the problem is that emergencies and wars are not mutually exclusive; so the existence of emergency powers in no way precludes the exercise of war powers. The attack on September 11 gave rise to an emergency and was followed by a war. No one disputes that the attack created emergency conditions within the United States. And both the UN Security Council and NATO recognized that al-Qaeda's acts constituted an "armed attack" justifying a military response in self-defense. After the Taliban government refused to arrest the al-Qaeda leaders, most nations supported the US attack in Afghanistan. Ackerman himself acknowledges that the conflict with Afghanistan was properly called a war. But if military force is an appropriate response to a catastrophic terrorist attack, there is no reason to believe that the existence of the additional emergency detention powers Ackerman proposes will do anything to reduce reliance on war powers or "war talk" after the attack takes place.

Ackerman contends that by providing short-term emergency measures, we will reduce the likelihood that terrorist attacks will lead to long-term losses of civil liberties. Without emergency powers, he argues, Congress will be tempted, as it was in the Patriot Act, to expand executive discretion permanently. But if the threat that terrorism poses is itself permanent—as Ackerman himself argues—it is not clear why only short-term changes are appropriate. While temporary preventive detention is certainly one way for a government to respond to terrorist threats, it is not the only or even the principal way. Since September 11, the Bush administration has, among other things, (1) reorganized the federal bureaucracy, (2) increased border and airport security, (3) reduced barriers to information sharing among law enforcement and intelligence officials, (4) prohibited the financing of terrorist organizations, (5) expanded prohibitions on money laundering, (6) sent undercover informants into mosques, (7) engaged in warrantless wiretapping of Americans, (8) prosecuted lawyers, translators, and Web site managers for speech, (9) detained "enemy combatants" at Guantánamo Bay, Bagram Air Force Base in Afghanistan, and in Iraq, (10) carried out "targeted assassinations" of al-Qaeda suspects, (11) created a network of secret detention centers around the world into which the government has "disappeared" other suspected al-Qaeda leaders, (12) employed coercive interrogation tactics up to and including torture, and (13) rendered other suspects to third countries to be tortured there. Ackerman offers no reason to think that giving the president the power to detain suspects without charges for forty-five days after the September 11 attacks would have forestalled any of these measures.

What is more, Ackerman quickly acknowledges that our amendment process makes all but the most uncontroversial constitutional amendments virtually impossible to enact, and that this is also true of his scheme for emergency powers. Instead, he proposes a "framework statute." But this in turn further diminishes any likelihood that Ackerman's plan would have any limiting effect on post-attack responses. Unlike a constitutional amendment, a statute would have no binding effect on subsequent Congresses. The Constitution gives Congress the power to enact or repeal any law within its authority, so long as it obtains a bare majority of each house and the approval of the president. If a majority of Congress believes that emergency conditions persist six months after an armed attack, but 21 percent of the Senate disagrees, nothing would stop the majority from repealing the requirement for larger and larger majorities—Ackerman's "supermajoritarian escalator"—or simply passing another law giving the president the same or even broader authorities.

Ackerman suggests that courts should strictly scrutinize any subsequent laws that undermine the "supermajoritarian escalator"; but if the escalator is only a statute, there would be no legal basis for doing so. When statutes conflict, the long-established rule is that the later statute prevails over the earlier, because Congress is always free to change its mind. At best, the existence of a statutory supermajoritarian escalator might have some persuasive but nonbinding effects on Congress; but if the pressures to act after a second or third catastrophic attack are as strong as Ackerman warns they will be, such precatory effects will not be nearly enough. For Ackerman's proposal to have any chance of limiting further damage to civil liberties, it would have to be a constitutional amendment—but as he concedes, that is not even within the realm of possibility.

Underlying Ackerman's proposal is a distrust of courts that is fashionable in the legal academy. Ackerman claims that judges cannot be relied upon during times of emergency, and that therefore it is better to place our bets on Congress. Ackerman criticizes at length the Supreme Court's treatment of Yaser Hamdi and José Padilla—US citizens designated as enemy combatants—to illustrate his point, but his arguments here are again unpersuasive. He castigates the Court, for example, for upholding the president's authority to detain Hamdi, a US citizen captured fighting for the enemy on the battlefield in Afghanistan, and he criticizes the Court for "balancing" Hamdi's rights against government claims based on security when it came to deciding what legal process was appropriate for him. But on the question of authority to detain Hamdi, Ackerman concedes that the US was at war in Afghanistan when Hamdi was captured, and he does not dispute that it is entirely routine—and lawful—for nations to detain those fighting for the enemy during wartime.

As for whether Hamdi was denied due process, the Court has long used a test that balances individual rights against security requirements to assess the appropriate procedures when the government claims preventive detention is necessary. It uses such a test in cases ranging from the detention of those awaiting criminal trial or immigration hearings to the "civil commitment" of mentally ill and dangerous citizens. In the absence of an absolute prohibition on preventive detention—something neither this country nor any other nation of which I am aware has ever accepted—it is difficult to see how else to assess appropriate procedures than by balancing, as the Court does in *Hamdi*, the detained person's rights against the government's security needs. One can certainly disagree with the particular balance the Court struck; but Ackerman's preventive detention procedure would offer even less protection to Hamdi's rights. The Court in *Hamdi* held that at an irreducible minimum, due process requires that a detainee have a meaningful opportunity to confront the charges against him before an impartial decision-maker; Ackerman's scheme would offer no opportunity whatever to challenge the basis for incarceration.

So Ackerman's criticisms are overblown. Moreover, he fails to acknowledge the most important feature of the Court's 2004 decisions about "enemy combatants"—their powerful refutation of the president's argument that his detention authority could not be subjected to any meaningful judicial review.

If the courts do not afford fully adequate protection, Congress is certainly no better. Hamdi and Padilla would both be in military detention today had the matter been left to Congress, which did nothing to protect either man during their many years behind bars, despite the fact that their treatment prompted probably the most widespread condemnation by lawyers and the public of any tactic used in the "war on terror," including even the torture at Abu Ghraib.

Ackerman is correct that those concerned with the demise of civil liberties need to offer credible alternatives to the administration's "war on terror." The conservative columnist David Brooks pithily captured the political reality in commenting on the January 2006 hearings on the nomination of Supreme Court Justice Samuel Alito. While Democratic senators had futilely pressed Alito on the law, the Republicans had insisted on the need for security. Brooks said, "You saw people like Lindsay Graham, a Republican, saying, 'I'm worried about terrorists.' You saw Democrats saying, 'I'm worried about the NSA.' That is a clear winner for the Republicans." In today's political climate, and certainly for this administration, security often takes precedence over law. If they are to get national political support, liberals must offer sensible security proposals that are consistent with basic principles of the rule of law.

But Ackerman's alternative is not sensible.[4] That he goes to such lengths as to suggest an "Emergency Constitution" authorizing detention without charges may suggest to some that existing laws and procedures are inadequate to provide security in states of emergency. In fact, there is already a wide range of measures that are legal and appropriate in responding to a terrorist attack and seeking to prevent another attack. They include: increasing security at borders, airports, and other sites of potential attack, such as chemical plants; using military force, detentions, and trials, so long as they are consistent with the UN Charter and the laws of war; investigating potential terrorists pursuant to the Foreign Intelligence Surveillance Act; prosecuting those who conspire to engage in terrorist acts or aid or abet such acts; securing nuclear materials to keep them out of terrorists' hands; improving coordination between law enforcement and intelligence officials; increasing aid to foreign communities where poverty and

---

4. Those interested in a more empirical attempt to articulate an alternative national security vision would do well to read Harvard professors Philip Heymann and Juliette Kayyem's book, *Protecting Liberty in an Age of Terror* (MIT Press, 2005). Heymann and Kayyem, both of whom worked on national security issues in the Clinton Justice Department, consulted an impressively diverse range of national security experts, and offer recommendations on everything from domestic surveillance to coercive interrogation and targeted killings. While some of their recommendations, especially their proposal to authorize what they call "highly coercive interrogation" short of torture, are questionable, their approach is more comprehensive and more attentive to reality than Ackerman's.

resentment toward the US have been exploited by terrorists; reducing US dependence on oil to offset the perverse incentives that such dependence creates for American foreign policy; and making progress toward global disarmament. Such measures, and they are only a sample, would increase US security without necessarily undermining constitutional principles, and most significantly, without encouraging the rampant anti-Americanism that the Bush administration's disregard of the rule of law has exacerbated around the world.

In the end, Ackerman's book has a distinct air of unreality about it. He pleads eloquently for legislative reform now—"before the next attack." But the reality is that nothing substantial happens in Congress unless actual events and political pressures create a need for action. The September 11 attacks brought about widespread changes, some of them sensible and long-needed, others hasty and wrongheaded. The revelations of prisoner abuse at Abu Ghraib and elsewhere, coupled with the sustained attention afforded these issues by human rights groups and the press, led to the McCain Amendment, which reaffirmed that the prohibition on cruel, inhuman, and degrading treatment extends to all human beings everywhere—and not just to Americans or those held within the United States, as the Bush administration had secretly asserted. Similarly, political and legal challenges to Guantánamo have forced reforms there, including the introduction of hearings to determine the status of prisoners, reduced reliance on coercive interrogation tactics, and the release of over 250 detainees. At home, a concerted campaign by librarians and civil libertarians led to restrictions on the Patriot Act provision authorizing the seizure of library records in foreign intelligence investigations.

None of these reforms has been as effective or extensive as they should have been. Congress undercut the McCain Amendment by enacting another law that barred Guantánamo detainees from seeking any judicial protection if they are being subjected to torture. When President Bush signed the amendment, he attached a statement asserting that, as commander in chief, he had the power to violate it whenever he chose to do so. Despite the reforms at Guantánamo, the government is still holding many people there who pose no threat whatever to the US. The government itself has determined that only 8 percent of the Guantánamo detainees were fighters for al-Qaeda.[5] No high-level US official has been held responsible for the widespread pattern of torture and coercive interrogation revealed at Abu Ghraib, Guantánamo, and elsewhere. And earlier this year Congress reauthorized the Patriot Act without even discussing many of its most troubling provisions—such as those authorizing deportation of people for their political associations, and empowering the attorney general to lock up foreign nationals without charges.

But whether one stresses the progress made by those who care about civil liberties and the rule of law or the distance we still have to go to restore those values, there is, and will continue to be, a continuing political and legal struggle over the character of American democracy in the face of what is, in all likelihood, a permanent threat of catastrophic terrorism. Abstract pleas for structural reform, such as Ackerman's, are unlikely to have much effect without careful attention to the government's particular failures to protect rights and security. If remedies are to be taken seriously, they must be responsive to real needs. Ackerman's proposal fails not only because it is insufficiently thought through, but more fundamentally because it is disconnected from the reality of what is actually happening to people denied elementary rights.

---

5. Mark Denbeaux and Joshua W. Denbeaux, "Report on Guantánamo Detainees: A Profile of 517 Detainees Through Analysis of Department of Defense Data," February 2006, available at http://papers.ssrn.com/sol3/papers.cfm?abstract_id=885659.

Appendix

ON NSA SPYING:
A LETTER TO CONGRESS

DEAR MEMBERS OF CONGRESS:

We are scholars of constitutional law and former government officials. We write in our individual capacities as citizens concerned by the Bush administration's National Security Agency domestic spying program, as reported in *The New York Times*, and in particular to respond to the Justice Department's December 22, 2005, letter to the majority and minority leaders of the House and Senate Intelligence Committees setting forth the administration's defense of the program.[1] Although the program's secrecy prevents us from being privy to all of its details, the Justice Department's defense of what it concedes was secret and warrantless electronic surveillance of persons within the United States fails to identify any plausible legal authority for such surveillance. Accordingly the program appears on its face to violate existing law.

The basic legal question here is not new. In 1978, after an extensive investigation of the privacy violations associated with foreign intelligence surveillance programs, Congress and the President enacted the

---

1. The Justice Department letter can be found at www.nationalreview.com/pdf/12%2022%202005%20NSA%20letter.pdf.

Foreign Intelligence Surveillance Act (FISA). Pub. L. 95-511, 92 Stat. 1783. FISA comprehensively regulates electronic surveillance within the United States, striking a careful balance between protecting civil liberties and preserving the "vitally important government purpose" of obtaining valuable intelligence in order to safeguard national security. S. Rep. No. 95-604, pt. 1, at 9 (1977).

With minor exceptions, FISA authorizes electronic surveillance only upon certain specified showings, and only if approved by a court. The statute specifically allows for warrantless *wartime* domestic electronic surveillance—but only for the first fifteen days of a war. 50 U.S.C. § 1811. It makes criminal any electronic surveillance not authorized by statute, *id.* § 1809; and it expressly establishes FISA and specified provisions of the federal criminal code (which govern wiretaps for criminal investigation) as the "*exclusive* means by which electronic surveillance . . . may be conducted," 18 U.S.C. § 2511(2)(f) (emphasis added).[2]

The Department of Justice concedes that the NSA program was not authorized by any of the above provisions. It maintains, however, that the program did not violate existing law because Congress implicitly authorized the NSA program when it enacted the Authorization for Use of Military Force (AUMF) against al-Qaeda, Pub. L. No. 107-40, 115 Stat. 224 (2001). But the AUMF cannot reasonably be construed to implicitly authorize warrantless electronic surveillance in the United States during wartime, where Congress has expressly and specifically addressed that precise question in FISA and limited any such warrantless surveillance to the first fifteen days of war.

The DOJ also invokes the President's inherent constitutional authority as Commander in Chief to collect "signals intelligence" targeted at

---

2. More detail about the operation of FISA can be found in Congressional Research Service, "Presidential Authority to Conduct Warrantless Electronic Surveillance to Gather Foreign Intelligence Information" (January 5, 2006). This letter was drafted prior to release of the CRS Report, which corroborates the conclusions drawn here.

the enemy, and maintains that construing FISA to prohibit the President's actions would raise constitutional questions. But even conceding that the President in his role as Commander in Chief may generally collect "signals intelligence" on the enemy abroad, Congress indisputably has authority to regulate electronic surveillance within the United States, as it has done in FISA. Where Congress has so regulated, the President can act in contravention of statute only if his authority is exclusive, that is, not subject to the check of statutory regulation. The DOJ letter pointedly does not make that extraordinary claim.

Moreover, to construe the AUMF as the DOJ suggests would itself raise serious constitutional questions under the Fourth Amendment. The Supreme Court has never upheld warrantless wiretapping within the United States. Accordingly, the principle that statutes should be construed to avoid serious constitutional questions provides an additional reason for concluding that the AUMF does not authorize the President's actions here.

I.

Congress did not implicitly authorize the NSA domestic spying
program in the AUMF, and in fact expressly prohibited it in FISA

The DOJ concedes (Letter at 4) that the NSA program involves "electronic surveillance," which is defined in FISA to mean the interception of the *contents* of telephone, wire, or e-mail communications that occur, at least in part, in the United States. 50 U.S.C. §§ 1801(f)(1)-(2), 1801(n). The NSA engages in such surveillance without judicial approval, and apparently without the substantive showings that FISA requires—e.g., that the subject is an "agent of a foreign power." *Id.* § 1805(a). The DOJ does not argue that FISA itself authorizes such electronic surveillance; and, as the DOJ letter acknowledges, 18 U.S.C. § 1809 makes criminal any electronic surveillance not authorized by statute.

The DOJ nevertheless contends that the surveillance is authorized by the AUMF, signed on September 18, 2001, which empowers the President to use "all necessary and appropriate force against" al-Qaeda. According to the DOJ, collecting "signals intelligence" on the enemy, even if it involves tapping US phones without court approval or probable cause, is a "fundamental incident of war" authorized by the AUMF. This argument fails for four reasons.

First, and most importantly, the DOJ's argument rests on an unstated general "implication" from the AUMF that directly contradicts *express* and *specific* language in FISA. Specific and "carefully drawn" statutes prevail over general statutes where there is a conflict. *Morales v. TWA, Inc.*, 504 U.S. 374, 384-85 (1992) (quoting *International Paper Co. v. Ouelette*, 479 U.S. 481, 494 (1987)). In FISA, Congress has directly and specifically spoken on the question of domestic warrantless wiretapping, including during wartime, and it could not have spoken more clearly.

As noted above, Congress has comprehensively regulated all electronic surveillance in the United States, and authorizes such surveillance only pursuant to specific statutes designated as the "*exclusive* means by which electronic surveillance... and the interception of domestic wire, oral, and electronic communications may be conducted." 18 U.S.C. § 2511(2)(f) (emphasis added). Moreover, FISA *specifically* addresses the question of domestic wiretapping during wartime. In a provision entitled "Authorization during time of war," FISA dictates that "notwithstanding any other law, the President, through the Attorney General, may authorize electronic surveillance without a court order under this subchapter to acquire foreign intelligence information *for a period not to exceed fifteen calendar days following a declaration of war by the Congress.*" 50 U.S.C. § 1811 (emphasis added). Thus, even where Congress has declared war —a more formal step than an authorization such as the AUMF—the law limits warrantless wiretapping to the first fifteen days of the conflict. Congress explained that if the President needed further warrantless surveillance during wartime, the fifteen days would be sufficient for Congress to consider and enact further authorization.[3] Rather than follow this course, the President acted unilaterally and secretly in contravention of FISA's terms. The DOJ letter remarkably does not even *mention* FISA's fifteen-day war provision, which directly refutes the President's asserted "implied" authority.

In light of the specific and comprehensive regulation of FISA, especially the fifteen-day war provision, there is no basis for finding in the AUMF's general language implicit authority for unchecked warrantless domestic wiretapping. As Justice Frankfurter stated in rejecting a similar argument by President Truman when he sought to defend the seizure of the steel mills during the Korean War on the basis of implied congressional authorization:

> It is one thing to draw an intention of Congress from general language and to say that Congress would have explicitly written what is inferred, where Congress has not addressed itself to a specific situation. It is quite impossible, however, when Congress did specifically address itself to a problem, as Congress did to that of seizure, to find secreted in the interstices of legislation the very grant of power which Congress consciously withheld. To find authority so explicitly withheld is... to disrespect the whole legislative process and the constitutional division of authority between President and Congress. *Youngstown Sheet*

---

3. "The Conferees intend that this [15-day] period will allow time for consideration of any amendment to this act that may be appropriate during a wartime emergency.... The conferees expect that such amendment would be reported with recommendations within 7 days and that each House would vote on the amendment within 7 days thereafter." H.R. Conf. Rep. No. 95-1720, at 34 (1978).

& Tube Co. v. *Sawyer,* 343 U.S. 579, 609 (1952) (Frankfurter, J., concurring).

Second, the DOJ's argument would require the conclusion that Congress implicitly and *sub silentio* repealed 18 U.S.C. § 2511(2)(f), the provision that identifies FISA and specific criminal code provisions as "the exclusive means by which electronic surveillance... may be conducted." Repeals by implication are strongly disfavored; they can be established only by "overwhelming evidence," *J.E.M. Ag. Supply, Inc.* v. *Pioneer Hi-Bred Int'l, Inc.,* 534 U.S. 124, 137 (2001), and "'the only permissible justification for a repeal by implication is when the earlier and later statutes are irreconcilable,'" *id.* at 141–142 (quoting *Morton* v. *Mancari,* 417 U.S. 535, 550 (1974)). The AUMF and § 2511(2)(f) are not irreconcilable, and there is *no* evidence, let alone overwhelming evidence, that Congress intended to repeal § 2511(2)(f).

Third, Attorney General Alberto Gonzales has admitted that the administration did not seek to amend FISA to authorize the NSA spying program because it was advised that Congress would reject such an amendment.[4] The administration cannot argue on the one hand that Congress authorized the NSA program in the AUMF, and at the same time that it did not ask Congress for such authorization because it feared Congress would say no.[5]

---

4. Attorney General Gonzales stated, "We have had discussions with Congress in the past— certain members of Congress—as to whether or not FISA could be amended to allow us to adequately deal with this kind of threat, and we were advised that that would be difficult, if not impossible." Press Briefing by Attorney General Alberto Gonzales and General Michael Hayden, Principal Deputy Director for National Intelligence (December 19, 2005), available at www.whitehouse.gov/news/releases/2005/12/20051219-1.html.

5. The administration had a convenient vehicle for seeking any such amendment in the USA PATRIOT Act of 2001, Pub. L. No. 107-56, 115 Stat. 272, enacted in October 2001. The Patriot Act amended FISA in several respects, including in sections 218 (allowing FISA wiretaps in criminal investigations) and 215 (popularly known as the "libraries provision"). Yet the administration did not ask Congress to amend FISA to authorize the warrantless electronic surveillance at issue here.

Finally, the DOJ's reliance upon *Hamdi* v. *Rumsfeld*, 542 U.S. 507 (2004), to support its reading of the AUMF, see DOJ Letter at 3, is misplaced. A plurality of the Court in *Hamdi* held that the AUMF authorized military detention of enemy combatants captured on the battlefield abroad as a "fundamental incident of waging war." *Id.* at 519. The plurality expressly limited this holding to individuals who were "part of or supporting forces hostile to the United States or coalition partners *in Afghanistan and who engaged in an armed conflict against the United States there.*" *Id.* at 516 (emphasis added). It is one thing, however, to say that foreign battlefield capture of enemy combatants is an incident of waging war that Congress intended to authorize. It is another matter entirely to treat unchecked warrantless *domestic* spying as included in that authorization, especially where an existing statute specifies that other laws are the "exclusive means" by which electronic surveillance may be conducted and provides that even a declaration of war authorizes such spying only for a fifteen-day emergency period.[6]

---

6. The DOJ attempts to draw an analogy between FISA and 18 U.S.C. § 4001(a), which provides that the United States may not detain a US citizen "except pursuant to an act of Congress." The DOJ argues that just as the AUMF was deemed to authorize the detention of Hamdi, 542 U.S. at 519, so the AUMF satisfies FISA's requirement that electronic surveillance be "authorized by statute." DOJ Letter at 3–4. The analogy is inapt. As noted above, FISA specifically limits warrantless domestic wartime surveillance to the first fifteen days of the conflict, and 18 U.S.C. § 2511(2)(f) specifies that existing law is the "exclusive means" for domestic wiretapping. Section 4001(a), by contrast, neither expressly addresses detention of the enemy during wartime nor attempts to create an exclusive mechanism for detention. Moreover, the analogy overlooks the carefully limited holding and rationale of the Hamdi plurality, which found the AUMF to be an "explicit congressional authorization for the detention of individuals in the narrow category we describe... who fought against the United States in Afghanistan as part of the Taliban, an organization known to have supported the al Qaeda terrorist network," and whom "Congress sought to target in passing the AUMF." 542 U.S. at 518. By the government's own admission, the NSA program is by no means so limited. See Gonzales/Hayden Press Briefing, supra note 4.

2.

Construing FISA *to prohibit warrantless domestic wiretapping does not raise any serious constitutional question, while construing the* AUMF *to authorize such wiretapping would raise serious questions under the Fourth Amendment*

The DOJ argues that FISA and the AUMF should be construed to permit the NSA program's domestic surveillance because there otherwise might be a "conflict between FISA and the President's Article II authority as Commander-in-Chief." DOJ Letter at 4. The statutory scheme described above is not ambiguous, and therefore the constitutional avoidance doctrine is not even implicated. See *United States v. Oakland Cannabis Buyers' Coop.*, 532 U.S. 483, 494 (2001) (the "canon of constitutional avoidance has no application in the absence of statutory ambiguity"). But were it implicated, it would work against the President, not in his favor. Construing FISA and the AUMF according to their plain meanings raises no serious constitutional questions regarding the President's duties under Article II. Construing the AUMF to *permit* unchecked warrantless wiretapping without probable cause, however, would raise serious questions under the Fourth Amendment.

A. FISA*'s limitations are consistent with the President's Article II role*

We do not dispute that, absent congressional action, the President might have inherent constitutional authority to collect "signals intelligence" about the enemy abroad. Nor do we dispute that, had Congress taken no action in this area, the President might well be constitutionally empowered to conduct domestic surveillance directly tied and narrowly confined to that goal—subject, of course, to Fourth Amendment limits. Indeed, in the years before FISA was enacted, the federal law involving wiretapping specifically provided that "nothing contained in this chapter or in section 605 of the Communications Act of 1934 shall limit the constitutional power of the President... to obtain foreign intelligence information deemed essential to the security of the United States." 18 U.S.C. § 2511(3) (1976).

But FISA specifically *repealed* that provision, FISA § 201(c), 92 Stat. 1797, and replaced it with language dictating that FISA and the criminal code are the "exclusive means" of conducting electronic surveillance. In doing so, Congress did not deny that the President has constitutional power to conduct electronic surveillance for national security purposes; rather, Congress properly concluded that "even if the President has the inherent authority *in the absence of legislation* to authorize warrantless electronic surveillance for foreign intelligence purposes, Congress has the power to regulate the conduct of such surveillance by legislating a reasonable procedure, which then becomes the exclusive means by which such surveillance may be conducted." H.R. Rep. No. 95-1283, pt. 1, at 24 (1978) (emphasis added). This analysis, Congress noted, was "supported by two successive Attorneys General." *Id.*

To say that the President has inherent authority does not mean that his authority is exclusive, or that his conduct is not subject to statutory regulations enacted (as FISA was) pursuant to Congress's Article I powers. As Justice Jackson famously explained in his influential opinion in *Youngstown Sheet & Tube Co. v. Sawyer*, 343 U.S. at 635 (Jackson, J., concurring), the Constitution "enjoins upon its branches separateness but interdependence, autonomy but reciprocity. Presidential powers are not fixed but fluctuate, depending upon their disjunction or conjunction with those of Congress." For example, the President in his role as Commander in Chief directs military operations. But the Framers gave Congress the power to prescribe rules for the regulation of the armed and naval forces, Art. I, § 8, cl. 14, and if a duly enacted statute prohibits the military from engaging in torture or cruel, inhuman, and degrading treatment, the President must follow that dictate. As Justice Jackson wrote, when the President acts in defiance of "the expressed or implied will of Congress," his power is "at its lowest ebb." 343 U.S. at 637. In this setting, Jackson wrote, "Presidential power [is] most vulnerable to attack and in the least favorable of all constitutional postures." *Id.* at 640.

Congress plainly has authority to regulate domestic wiretapping by federal agencies under its Article I powers, and the DOJ does not suggest otherwise. Indeed, when FISA was enacted, the Justice Department agreed that Congress had power to regulate such conduct, and could require judicial approval of foreign intelligence surveillance.[7] FISA does not prohibit foreign intelligence surveillance, but merely imposes reasonable regulation to protect legitimate privacy rights. (For example, although FISA generally requires judicial approval for electronic surveillance of persons within the United States, it permits the executive branch to install a wiretap immediately so long as it obtains judicial approval within seventy-two hours. 50 U.S.C. § 1805(f).)

Just as the President is bound by the statutory prohibition on torture, he is bound by the statutory dictates of FISA.[8] The DOJ once infamously argued that the President as Commander in Chief could

---

7. See, e.g., S. Rep. No. 95-604, pt. I, at 16 (1977) (Congress's assertion of power to regulate the President's authorization of electronic surveillance for foreign intelligence purposes was "concurred in by the Attorney General"); Foreign Intelligence Electronic Surveillance: Hearings Before the Subcomm. on Legislation of the House Permanent Select Comm. on Intelligence, 95th Cong., 2d Sess., at 31 (1978) (Letter from John M. Harmon, Assistant Attorney General, Office of Legal Counsel, to Edward P. Boland, Chairman, House Permanent Select Comm. on Intelligence (Apr. 18, 1978)) ("it seems unreasonable to conclude that Congress, in the exercise of its powers in this area, may not vest in the courts the authority to approve intelligence surveillance").

8. Indeed, Article II imposes on the President the general obligation to enforce laws that Congress has validly enacted, including FISA: "he shall take Care that the Laws be faithfully executed..." (emphasis added). The use of the mandatory "shall" indicates that under our system of separation of powers, he is duty-bound to execute the provisions of FISA, not defy them.

ignore even the criminal prohibition on torture,[9] and, more broadly still, that statutes may not "place *any* limits on the President's determinations as to any terrorist threat, the amount of military force to be used in response, or the method, timing, and nature of the response."[10] But the administration withdrew the August 2002 torture memo after it was disclosed, and for good reason the DOJ does not advance these extreme arguments here. Absent a serious question about FISA's constitutionality, there is no reason even to consider construing the AUMF to have implicitly overturned the carefully designed regulatory regime that FISA establishes. See, e.g., *Reno v. Flores*, 507 U.S. 292, 314 n.9 (1993) (constitutional avoidance canon applicable only if the constitutional question to be avoided is a serious one, "not to eliminate all possible contentions that the statute *might* be unconstitutional") (emphasis in original; citation omitted).[11]

---

9. See Memorandum from Jay S. Bybee, Assistant Attorney General, Department of Justice Office of Legal Counsel, to Alberto R. Gonzales, Counsel to the President, Re: *Standards of Conduct for Interrogation under 18 U.S.C. §§ 2340-2340A* (Aug. 1, 2002), at 31.

10. Memorandum from John C. Yoo, Deputy Assistant Attorney General, Office of Legal Counsel, to the Deputy Counsel to the President, Re: *The President's Constitutional Authority to Conduct Military Operations Against Terrorists and Nations Supporting Them* (September 25, 2001), available at www.usdoj.gov/olc/warpowers925.htm (emphasis added).

11. Three years ago, the FISA Court of Review suggested in dictum that Congress cannot "encroach on the President's constitutional power" to conduct foreign intelligence surveillance. In re Sealed Case No. 02-001, 310 F.3d 717, 742 (FIS Ct. Rev. 2002) (per curiam). The FISA Court of Review, however, did not hold that FISA was unconstitutional, nor has any other court suggested that FISA's modest regulations constitute an impermissible encroachment on presidential authority. The FISA Court of Review relied upon *United States v. Truong Dihn Hung*, 629 F.2d 908 (4th Cir. 1980)—but that court did not suggest that the President's powers were beyond congressional control. To the contrary, the *Truong* court indicated that FISA's restrictions were constitutional. 629 F.2d at 915 n.4 (noting that "the imposition of a warrant requirement, beyond the constitutional minimum described in this opinion, *should be left to the intricate balancing performed in the course of the legislative process by Congress and the President*") (emphasis added).

B. Construing the AUMF to authorize warrantless domestic wiretapping would raise serious constitutional questions

The principle that ambiguous statutes should be construed to avoid serious constitutional questions works against the administration, not in its favor. Interpreting the AUMF and FISA to permit unchecked domestic wiretapping for the duration of the conflict with al-Qaeda would certainly raise serious constitutional questions. The Supreme Court has never upheld such a sweeping power to invade the privacy of Americans at home without individualized suspicion or judicial oversight.

The NSA surveillance program permits wiretapping within the United States without *either* of the safeguards presumptively required by the Fourth Amendment for electronic surveillance—individualized probable cause and a warrant or other order issued by a judge or magistrate. The Court has long held that wiretaps generally require a warrant and probable cause. *Katz* v. *United States*, 389 U.S. 347 (1967). And the only time the Court considered the question of national security wiretaps, it held that the Fourth Amendment prohibits domestic security wiretaps without those safeguards. *United States* v. *United States District Court*, 407 U.S. 297 (1972). Although the Court in that case left open the question of the Fourth Amendment validity of warrantless wiretaps for foreign intelligence purposes, its precedents raise serious constitutional questions about the kind of open-ended authority the President has asserted with respect to the NSA program. See *id.* at 316-18 (explaining difficulty of guaranteeing Fourth Amendment freedoms if domestic surveillance can be conducted solely in the discretion of the executive branch).

Indeed, serious Fourth Amendment questions about the validity of warrantless wiretapping led Congress to enact FISA, in order to "provide the secure framework by which the executive branch may conduct legitimate electronic surveillance for foreign intelligence purposes within the context of this nation's commitment to privacy and individual rights."

S. Rep. No. 95-604, at 15 (1978) (citing, *inter alia, Zweibon v. Mitchell,* 516 F.2d 594 (D.C. Cir. 1975), *cert. denied,* 425 U.S. 944 (1976), in which the court of appeals held that a warrant must be obtained before a wiretap is installed on a domestic organization that is neither the agent of, nor acting in collaboration with, a foreign power).

Relying on *In re Sealed Case No. 02-001,* the DOJ argues that the NSA program falls within an exception to the warrant and probable cause requirement for reasonable searches that serve "special needs" above and beyond ordinary law enforcement. But the existence of "special needs" has never been found to permit warrantless wiretapping. "Special needs" generally excuse the warrant and individualized suspicion requirements only where those requirements are impracticable and the intrusion on privacy is minimal. See, e.g., *Griffin v. Wisconsin,* 483 U.S. 868, 873 (1987). Wiretapping is not a minimal intrusion on privacy, and the experience of FISA shows that foreign intelligence surveillance can be carried out through warrants based on individualized suspicion.

The court in *Sealed Case* upheld FISA itself, which requires warrants issued by Article III federal judges upon an individualized showing of probable cause that the subject is an "agent of a foreign power." The NSA domestic spying program, by contrast, includes none of these safeguards. It does not require individualized judicial approval, and it does not require a showing that the target is an "agent of a foreign power." According to Attorney General Gonzales, the NSA may wiretap any person in the United States who so much as receives a communication from anyone abroad, if the administration deems either of the parties to be affiliated with al-Qaeda, a member of an organization affiliated with al-Qaeda, "working in support of al Qaeda," or "part of" an organization or group "that is supportive of al Qaeda."[12] Under this reasoning, a US citizen living here who

---

12. See Gonzales/Hayden Press Briefing, *supra* note 4.

received a phone call from another US citizen who attends a mosque that the administration believes is "supportive" of al-Qaeda could be wiretapped without a warrant. The absence of meaningful safeguards on the NSA program at a minimum raises serious questions about the validity of the program under the Fourth Amendment, and therefore supports an interpretation of the AUMF that does not undercut FISA's regulation of such conduct.

In conclusion, the DOJ letter fails to offer a plausible legal defense of the NSA domestic spying program. If the administration felt that FISA was insufficient, the proper course was to seek legislative amendment, as it did with other aspects of FISA in the Patriot Act, and as Congress expressly contemplated when it enacted the wartime wiretap provision in FISA. One of the crucial features of a constitutional democracy is that it is always open to the President—or anyone else—to seek to change the law. But it is also beyond dispute that, in such a democracy, the President cannot simply violate criminal laws behind closed doors because he deems them obsolete or impracticable.[13]

We hope you find these views helpful to your consideration of the legality of the NSA domestic spying program.

---

13. During consideration of FISA, the House of Representatives noted, "The decision as to the standards governing when and how foreign intelligence electronic surveillance should be conducted is and should be a political decision ... properly made by the political branches of Government together, not adopted by one branch on its own and with no regard for the other. Under our Constitution legislation is the embodiment of just such political decisions." H.R. Conf. Rep. No. 95-1283, pt. 1, at 21-22.

Attorney General Griffin Bell supported FISA in part because "no matter how well intentioned or ingenious the persons in the Executive branch who formulate these measures, the crucible of the legislative process will ensure that the procedures will be affirmed by that branch of government which is more directly responsible to the electorate." Foreign Intelligence Surveillance Act of 1978: Hearings Before the Subcommittee on Intelligence and the Rights of Americans of the Senate Select Committee on Intelligence, 95th Cong., 2d Sess. 12 (1997).

Curtis Bradley, Duke Law School, former Counselor on International Law in the State Department Legal Adviser's Office[14]

David Cole, Georgetown University Law Center

Walter Dellinger, Duke Law School, former Deputy Assistant Attorney General, Office of Legal Counsel and Acting Solicitor General

Ronald Dworkin, NYU Law School

Richard Epstein, University of Chicago Law School, Senior Fellow, Hoover Institution

Philip B. Heymann, Harvard Law School, former Deputy Attorney General

Harold Hongju Koh, Dean, Yale Law School, former Assistant Secretary of State for Democracy, Human Rights and Labor, former Attorney-Adviser, Office of Legal Counsel, DOJ

Martin Lederman, Georgetown University Law Center, former Attorney-Adviser, Office of Legal Counsel, DOJ

Beth Nolan, former Counsel to the President and Deputy Assistant Attorney General, Office of Legal Counsel

William S. Sessions, former Director, FBI, former Chief United States District Judge

Geoffrey Stone, Professor of Law and former Provost, University of Chicago

Kathleen Sullivan, Professor and former Dean, Stanford Law School

Laurence H. Tribe, Harvard Law School

William Van Alstyne, William & Mary Law School, former Justice Department attorney

---

14. Affiliations are noted for identification purposes only.

Sources

Earlier versions of the essays in this book appeared as follows:

Chapter 1: *The New York Review of Books*, July 19, 2007

Chapter 2: *The New York Review of Books*, November 17, 2005

Chapter 3: *The New York Review of Books*, December 6, 2007

Chapter 4: *The New York Review of Books*, August 10, 2006

Chapter 5: *The New York Review of Books*, November 18, 2004

Chapter 6: *The New York Review of Books*, March 9, 2006

Chapter 7: *The New York Review of Books*, November 16, 2006

Chapter 8: *The New York Review of Books*, July 13, 2006

Appendix: *The New York Review of Books*, February 9, 2006